Basics Of Radio Control Airplanes

by L.F.Randolph

ABOUT THE AUTHOR

L.F. RANDOLPH

"Randy" Randolph started modeling in 1934 and says he's been "at it" ever since. A long-time monthly contributor to *Model Airplane News,* Randy has won trophies in almost every model airplane event, including U-control, outdoor and indoor free-flight, pattern and scale. He also won the first Clipper Cargo event at the Nationals.

He has been a "ham" radio operator for more than 40 years; he built all his own equipment; and he even wrote a technical column for a ham publication for a while. When Randy built his first R/C aircraft in 1951, he designed not only the airplane, but also the radio.

To make a living, he ran his own food brokerage company, advertising agency and a small importing company. He now describes himself as a "retired gentleman of leisure who tries to meet editors' deadlines and build model airplanes."

Now living in Dallas, TX, Randy is old enough to have acquired nine grandchildren and three great-grandchildren. In this book, he shares his knowledge and years of experience with those who want to start building and flying model airplanes.

Chairman of the Board: Aldo DeFrancesco
President and CEO: Louis DeFrancesco Jr.
Senior Vice President: Yvonne M. DeFrancesco
Art Director: Alan Palermo
Book Design: Brett Eric Newman
Cover Design: Betty K. Nero
Art Assistant: Stephanie Warzecha
Copy Director: Lynne Sewell
Copy Editors: Katherine Tolliver,
Li Agen, Brenda J. Casey
Technical Editor: Richard Uravitch
Systems Assistant: Jackie Mosier

INTRODUCTION

Are you looking for a way to escape the tensions of modern life? Do you want to do something that's not only enjoyable, but also challenging and satisfying? Try building and flying R/C model airplanes.

This book contains information from "The Basics of R/C," which is a column I write for *Model Airplane News* magazine. You'll find basic information on how to get started—everything from the selection of an airplane to how to maintain and repair it. All the techniques outlined apply to scratch-building and to building with kits, and although aerodynamics is beyond the scope of this book, there are some rule-of-thumb-type calculations that you might find useful.

Building the most complicated model is a combination of many small tasks; some are as simple as cutting a piece of wood to the proper length; others are more difficult—but less difficult when you know how. I hope my years of modeling experience will help you get airborne quickly, and with minimum frustration! Who knows? This book may change your life!

Contents

ON THE COVER: All the airplanes shown on the cover can be built using the information contained in this book. From trainer to giant-scaler, each is the product of the knowledge and application of "basic" techniques. From the almost-ready-to-fly Global Hobbies Skylark 40 trainer (top), to the first flight (lower left) and the busy scale fly-in, all these airplanes embody the methods described in this book. Kodachromes by *Model Airplane News staff*.

Basic tools & basic terms

Instruction manuals don't always include the most basic information, and you won't be able to follow even the most elementary manual if you don't know about basic tools and the terms we use in aeromodeling. This section will help you.

Basic Tools

The photos show the minimum tools necessary. In one photo, the larger handle holds a blade that's made of half a single-edge razor blade. The other blade is a standard no. 11 that's available in all hobby stores. Pins should be of steel and not ball-point.

I made the sanding blocks in the other photo by wrapping various grades of sandpaper around 1-foot lengths of 1x2-inch pine block. Sharp pencils, straightedges, and right triangles form the remainder of the basic kit.

In Chapter 15, you'll learn more about the tools you'll need for modeling.

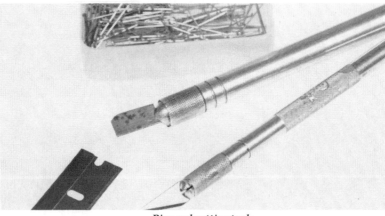

Pins and cutting tools.

Glossary

Aileron - A movable surface at the trailing edge of a wing; it controls the aircraft around the roll axis.

Airfoil - A cross-section view of a wing taken at right angles to its span and perpendicular to its plane. The rib section.

Angle of attack - The vertical angle at which the plane of a wing meets the air while in flight; controlled by the elevator.

Angle of incidence - The fixed vertical angle the plane of the wing forms with the horizontal center line of the fuselage.

Aspect ratio - The ratio of the wingspan to the wing chord (width). The number of times the width can be divided into the span.

Balance point - The point on the wing or fuselage where the airplane is in fore and aft and lateral balance. Don't confuse this with center of gravity.

Bellcrank - A lever with its fulcrum at the apex of the angle formed by its two arms. Allows pushrod movement to change direction.

Bulkhead - A former made of balsa or plywood that establishes the cross section of a fuselage at a specific location.

Camber - The mean distance between the top and the bottom of an airfoil from the leading to the trailing edge.

Center of gravity - The center of mass of an airplane. Usually abbreviated as CG.

Center of pressure - An imaginary point on the top of a wing where the lift can be considered to center at a given time.

Clevis - A U-shaped yoke on the end of a pushrod that connects it to a movable surface via a control horn.

Dihedral - The upward slant of a wing panel from the center to the tips.

Downthrust - The tilt of the engine and propeller downward in relation to the center line of the fuselage.

Elevator - The hinged surface on the horizontal tail that controls the fore and aft trim of an airplane.

Fillet - A fairing or smoothing of one surface into another for the purpose of reducing air resistance (drag).

Fin - The forward, or fixed, part of the vertical tail.

Firewall - The bulkhead (usually of plywood) that's immediately behind the engine and to which the engine is attached.

Fuselage - The body of an airplane.

Jig - A fixture that holds two or more parts in alignment during assembly.

Leading edge - The front edge of a wing or tail.

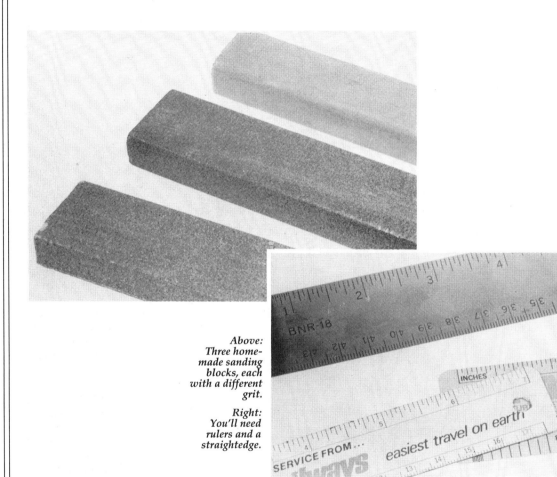

Above: Three home-made sanding blocks, each with a different grit.

Right: You'll need rulers and a straightedge.

Longeron - The main fore and aft members of a fuselage.

Nyrod - A system of flexible pushrods in which one moves freely inside the other. They are permanently attached to the structure of the airplane.

Pitch - The calculated distance, in inches, that a propeller will move forward in one revolution.

Planform - The outline of a wing or tail when viewed from above.

Rib - The cross-sectional wing member that maintains the shape of the airfoil.

Root - The part of a wing or tail that's nearest to its center

Servo - A radio-actuated, motor-driven device that imparts move-ment to a controlling device or a surface through a system of pushrods or bellcranks.

Spars - The span-wise load-bearing members of a wing or tail to which the ribs are attached.

Stability - The ability of an airplane to remain in level flight and return to it if disturbed.

Stall - The complete loss of lift caused by operating a wing at too high an angle of attack.

Sweep-back - The angling back of the leading edge of a wing or tail from the center to the tips.

Template - A pattern made from card stock or metal; it's used to duplicate parts.

Torque rod - A device that trans-mits movement along a longitudi-nal axis by a twisting motion.

Trailing edge - The rear edge of a wing or tail.

Wash-in - The twist imparted to a wing; it causes the tip to be at a higher angle of attack than the center.

Washout - The twist made in a wing; it causes the tip to be at a lower angle of attack than the center. ■

All airplanes are created equal...aren't they?

You can predict an aircraft's performance before you even build it! Eliminate surprises and increase your enjoyment of the sport by anticipating the effects of a change in size, wing, or fuselage configuration, and estimate the performance of kits from a variety of manufacturers.

Once we've mastered a basic trainer, most of us want to move on to aircraft with a higher performance. Good sense tells us that a multi-engine scale B-24 isn't a wise choice for us, but a less dramatic change can be almost as traumatic! An airplane can look like a trainer but behave very differently; for instance, its stalling speed could be the same as the friendly basic trainer's cruising speed, and this would make it a real handful to land. Appearances can deceive, so we need other ways to estimate performance characteristics.

The type of plane provides some information: pattern planes, racers and scale aircraft are all designed to perform according to the standards set for their class.

Pattern planes should fly at a constant speed, regardless of attitude, and they should respond smoothly and predictably to control input.

Racers do one thing—go fast. Their control surfaces move only minimally, so they won't cause drag and slow the airplane.

Scale planes are designed to fly like their counterparts; if the full-scale version is easy to fly, the scale reproduction probably will be, too!

Sport planes can vary widely in performance. Some fly slowly, others fly fast, and some do both. This class can include anything from a powered glider to a semi-bullet! Since sports are supposedly designed to meet the abilities of most modelers, trainers fall into this broad category.

It's obvious that describing an airplane as a "sport model" doesn't tell us much, and there are fortunately other ways to compare aircraft. They involve some arithmetic...but it's easy.

Wing loading is an excellent judging criteria. To calculate how much weight the wing must lift with its area, follow these steps:
● Multiply the wingspan (length) by the wing chord (width).
● Divide the answer by 144 to reduce it to square feet.
● Divide that answer (the wing area) into the airplane's total weight, in ounces.
The result is the wing loading in ounces per square foot.

If the wing has a constant chord, i.e., it's the same width from fuselage to tip, it's easy to calculate the wing area; but if the wing tapers, you must figure out the average chord. Do this by adding the chord measurement at the fuselage to that at the tip-rib station and dividing by 2. (*Other methods are given in the table.*)

If your trainer is in the 8- to 12-ounces-per-square-foot range, you should be able to handle an airplane with a 16-ounce loading.

Power loading is another good factor by which to judge performance. It stands to reason that if two airplanes have the same wing size but one weighs more than the other, the heavier one will need more power to stay in the air, as it must fly faster to stay airborne. More

Sport airplanes come in all shapes and sizes. Powered by a .40 4-stroke engine, this one has a high power-to-weight ratio as well as a low wing loading—things that make for good flight performance.

Left:This airplane is powered by a 2-cycle engine; it has relatively high wing and power loadings; and it flies fast. It's a handful for a beginner, but it looks like a trainer.

Below:This electric-powered sport model has low wing and power loadings combined with a relatively long tail arm and large stab. It flies like a powered glider—very gentle response to all controls.

speed requires more power. Power loading is usually expressed in horsepower per pound, but since horsepower is difficult to gauge, we'll divide the weight of the airplane by the engine's piston displacement in cubic inches.

If your trainer has a power loading in the 15-pounds-per-cubic-inch range and you move to an airplane with a higher wing loading, the power loading should be correspondingly *lower* in pounds per cubic inch —about 14 or 13 in the previous example.

If you enjoy arithmetic, you can use other factors to compare airplanes: aspect ratio, longitudinal dihedral, nose- and tail-moment arms, stab and rudder areas and— the most important—stability and proper balance point. ■

TABLE
Some Formulas To Remember

Power loading = Total weight (pounds)/Engine disp. (cubic inches)

Wing loading = Total weight (ounces)/Wing area (square feet)

Wing area = Wingspan x Average wing chord

Aspect ratio = Wingspan/Average wing chord

Average chord = Wing area/Wingspan
OR
Average chord = Square root of area/Aspect ratio

Average chord of a biplane =
$$\frac{\text{Chord (upper) x Area (upper) + Chord (lower) x Area (lower)}}{\text{Area (upper)} \mp \text{Area (lower)}}$$

What to look for

What's the best training airplane? If you ask the average R/Cer, nine times out of 10, he'll describe the first airplane that he could fly without that "sweaty hands" feeling! It may not have been his first trainer, but it was the first aircraft he could really fly. That's a clue to what a trainer should be—an airplane that becomes comfortable to fly.

Almost every R/C model manufacturer offers a "trainer." In many cases, the term is applied to any sport-type airplane! Sport planes can be used as trainers, but the term is often used as a sales tool and describes a relatively uncomplicated airplane—and a trainer should be uncomplicated.

Some fliers keep their first airplane for years, but as a rule, while we're learning, we all try something that's a little beyond our ability. Most of the time, we get away with it and learn, but sometimes we don't! This gives us another clue: your first trainer should be expendable, i.e., inexpensive!

The size of the plane is important, too. People who have good eyesight can easily see a small .049-powered airplane 1,000 feet in the air, while those of us who see the world through bifocals would be much more comfortable with a 6- or 7-footer at that altitude. A trainer should be large enough to see.

Color is also important. I have a friend who completely covered a nice airplane with chrome MonoKote, but it disappeared against the cloudy sky! The next time it came to the field, large areas had been trimmed in red and orange! Some colors are much easier to see than others, e.g., yellows, oranges and reds. Your trainer's color scheme should be visible rather than beautiful!

Get Comfortable

A "comfortable" airplane should have a wing loading between 10 and 15 ounces per square foot of wing area. To find the wing area, multiply the average width (chord) by the length (span). These measurements are usually given in inches, so divide the result by 144 to arrive at square feet. To derive the wing loading, divide the plane's weight (in ounces) by the wing area (in square feet). This is one way to

A typical training airplane, this PT-20 is a high-wing, 3-channel machine that's properly powered for its size and wing loading. This configuration has become almost standard for trainers.

predict an airplane's performance!

Engine displacement to airplane weight should be near the following guidelines. (Lower values are even better.)

.049s.....................up to $1^1/_2$ pounds
.10 to .15...............about 3 pounds
.20 to .30...............up to 4 pounds
.40 to .60...............5 to 6 pounds

To get an idea of what to look for in an airplane, compare these weights with the suggested wing-loading figures above. Most of the information you'll need is listed on the kit box.

Avoid complicated scale airplanes and radios with lots of additional features that can complicate learning. A few hobby dealers will sell you almost anything to make a profit (or to move hard-to-sell merchandise), and a $700 or

Trainers don't have to have a high wing. If they're not overpowered or over-weight, properly designed low-wing airplanes make excellent trainers.

$800 sale looks better to them than a satisfied, long-time customer. A good engine, an airplane and a 4- to 6-channel radio should cost no more than $300 to $400. The radio and engine, which are the most expensive items, are good investments; they'll fly new models for years to come!

Everyone has his own opinion of trainers, but everyone agrees that you should have flight instruction! Your local R/C club is a good place to look. You'll want to postpone that inevitable first crash for as long as possible! ∎

Model Airplane News' Twiliter is one of the best choices for someone who must learn to fly without an instructor. With the propeller removed and the engine covered with a plastic bag, it serves as a hand-launched glider.

They're making a comeback!

I'M NOT SURE OF the date of the first flight of a true, gas-powered model airplane, but it must have been early in the '20s. By today's standards, its engine was large and heavy, and free-flight models (R/C was still a long way off) were also large.

Gas model engines became practical in the mid '30s—their size being usually in the region of .60 cubic inch. Just before WW II, smaller engines became popular, and after the war, the trend was to smaller and smaller ones. The precision tooling developed for war production was used for civilian use, and model engines became readily available—especially the .049s, of which many millions were produced.

Big engines and airplanes are now making a comeback. The number of excellent kits increases each year, and in many cases, the larger size of their parts makes these planes easier to assemble, but the real reason for their popularity is their solid performance.

Wing size. The amount of lift that a wing will generate is proportional to its size, but not directly proportional! There's a scale factor involved, e.g., under certain conditions, a small wing (2 square feet) might generate 1 pound of lift, i.e., 8 ounces per square foot. Under similar conditions, a wing of 10 square feet with a similar shape might generate 10 pounds of lift, or 1 pound per square foot of area. That's twice as much per square foot as the smaller wing! The difference is in the volume of air that passes over the wing. Although the example is somewhat exaggerated, it does show that we can scale-down airplanes but not air!

Engine size. The larger the airplane, the larger the engine it requires. A larger wing provides more lift, but its increased drag requires more power to pull it through the air.

Some think that smaller engines require much more precision in their manufacture than larger engines, but this isn't true. A look at a plant that produces "giant-scale" engines shows the efforts made to produce efficient engines at a reasonable cost.

In its Texas plant, A&M Aircraft Inc. uses only CNC (Computer Numeric Control) machine tools to produce the parts for its large model engines. With the exception of cylinder and piston assemblies, which are pro-

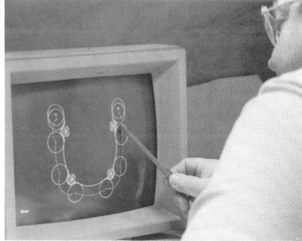

Top: Giant-scale Cub settles in for a landing. Big airplanes fly beautifully; many modelers will fly nothing else.

Above: Computer-controlled machines need programs to make them work. Al Willart explains a milling-machine program that makes the outside cuts on a crankcase.

duced elsewhere, all parts are machined by computerized tools that can hold a tolerance of .00005 inch. This level of precision ensures the proper fit of all parts in the finished product. This is the secret of good engine performance, and it's particularly true of engines made for $1/4$-scalers.

Apparent speed. Large airplanes seem to fly more slowly than smaller airplanes—"seems" is the key word. If an airplane is 2 feet long and flying at 30mph, it will take about .06 second for all of it to pass a given point; a 4-foot airplane will take .12 second to fly past that point at the same speed. Since our eyes focus on the whole airplane, the larger airplane seems to fly past more slowly.

Now move the larger airplane away until it seems to be the same size as the smaller airplane, and it really seems to slow down! This apparent speed differential, and the fact that larger machines have more inertia to overcome when control commands are given, contribute to the grace of their flight. They aren't necessarily easier to fly than smaller ones, but these characteristics do tend to lengthen the response time required to change flight attitudes.

Stability. Larger airplanes are less affected by wind gusts, updrafts and downdrafts because of the aforementioned inertia. This characteristic is important if your flying area is often windy.

Radio systems. Although transmitters and receivers don't vary according to the size of the airplane, the servos and associated hardware in large airplanes are subjected to greater flight loads than those in smaller birds. Big airplanes need big, powerful servos like the Futaba FPS134, or redundant servos (two on the same sur-

A finished crankcase that results from the program shown on the computer. These machines can easily hold tolerances of .0001 inch and, if necessary, .00005!

Big airplanes need big engines. This 4.6-cubic-inch job is by A&M Aircraft Inc.

face) and larger battery packs.

Hardware. Clevises, ball links and rod ends should be of the 4-40 threaded variety; control horns and bellcranks should also be heavy-duty; and control cables in a pull-pull arrangement with double control horns should replace pushrods.

Large models resemble full-scale planes more closely than other types of models, and $1/4$- or giant-scale airplanes aren't for everyone.

Expense, transportation difficulties, and having enough room for construction and storage are important considerations, but if you have more time and enough money, the "biggies" bring definite rewards in performance.

Should you start with a big bird? No; they aren't suitable as trainers, because inexperienced fliers crash frequently, and large airplanes cost more to repair. Learn to fly the little ones first! ■

Are they a wise choice for a new flier?

Model airplanes that are replicas of full-scale aircraft appeal to everyone. The clean, light planes of today, the glamorous planes of the '30s and the military birds of WW I and II have a charm that's easily understood.

This Stearman in the photograph is by Gary Pannell, and it's a good example of a scale model at its best. It's an exact reproduction of a plane Gary owned and flew for a number of years. Gary is an expert R/C pilot and has flown in just about every competition category from pattern to racing—and that's what it takes to fly a scale airplane!

In the early days of modeling when balsa was becoming the main construction material and models were all free flying, most kits were rubber-powered models of full-scale aircraft. There were a few exceptions—such as the competition types that were designed strictly for endurance—but scale kits were most popular with sport modelers. Most of the kits' boxes proclaimed their contents as "A Flying Model Airplane" and, in truth, they could be made to fly a little, but the flight achieved by the average modeler was more like that of a butterfly than an airplane!

Gas-Powered Models

With the development of the gas-powered model airplane engine, scale-type models started to lose their attraction for sport modelers. The reason was simply that a gas-powered model represented a large investment in time and money, and scale models of contemporary aircraft didn't fly well enough to justify the investment. They just didn't last long enough! Gas power was the way to go, and the emphasis was on flying, not on building and rebuilding.

U-Control Flight

Just before World War II, U-control made an appearance, and because of the stabilizing effect of the wires and the way they allowed pilots to control the attitude of an aircraft, scale

Is the pilot in the cockpit or on the ground with a transmitter in his hand? Gary Pannell's Stearman is a perfect example of a scale model.

models regained some of their previous popularity. They could be made to fly satisfactorily as long as they could be controlled. The "sport" model still prevailed because it flew better and, after all, flying was the whole idea!

Radio Control

In the early days of R/C flight, practically no consideration was given to scale models. The first radio equipment was crude and unreliable, and only the rudder was actuated by the radio, so the model had to be able to care for itself most of the time. This called for a stable, free-flying airplane, and scaled-down replicas of full-size airplanes just wouldn't work. As the radio equipment improved, the ability to fly scale-type models also improved and, as in U-control, they've now become an integral part of the R/C hobby/sport.

ARF Kits

ARF (Almost Ready to Fly) kits of scale airplanes are attractive, easy to assemble and offer a finished product that gives a great deal of satisfaction. But, they're not easy to fly. In the hands of an experienced pilot, they perform very well, but in the hands of a novice, the success rate is rather low (even with the help of an instructor).

So should you choose a scale model for your first plane? Everyone should build and fly at least one scale model, but not for a first attempt at flying. When you're skilled at flying, the sleek, scale beauty that has been a dream for years can become a reality. ∎

Try drawing your own

The plans that come with most R/C airplane kits are masterpieces of draftsmanship and art. They're arranged to help you with a step-by-step assembly sequence so that nothing is left out. Instruction manuals fill in any information gaps that might cause confusion during assembly. Kit manufacturers go to great lengths and expense to help you build a finished product of which you—and they—can be proud, but you don't really need extensive plans to build a model airplane.

Naturally, the construction of model airplanes differs from that of full-scale planes in many ways, including in the use of plans. In full-scale aircraft manufacturing, the plan is used to produce a jig in which the aircraft is assembled; in building model aircraft, the plans are the jigs. The relationship of the various sub-assemblies to one another is very important; therefore, the accuracy of the drawings is paramount.

Accurate construction comes from accurate drawings, and accurate drawings are made with the assistance of a few simple, inexpen-

These simple drafting tools—triangles, metal straightedge and T-square—make it easy to produce construction drawings for model airplanes.

sive tools that anyone can learn to use properly. Aside from a pencil and a drawing board, for accurate drawing, you'll need: a T-square, a metal yardstick and a set of triangles.

The plans for a constant-chord wing are made of intersecting vertical and horizontal lines. The horizontal lines indicate spars and leading and trailing edges; the vertical lines represent ribs.

To draw a plan for this simple wing, place the short bar of the T-square along the right edge of the drawing board so that it slides up and down along the edge and is in full contact with it at all times. The blade of the T-square is the base horizontal reference for all drawing.

Vertical lines are drawn with the aid of the triangles. Both triangles have one 90-degree (right) angle, but one has two 45-degree angles, and the other has a 60- and 30-degree configuration. These triangles can be combined to form a number of different angles but, for drawing our wing, only the 60/30 will be used.

Just a few lines are necessary to provide the jig on which to build the wing. Using masking tape or cellophane tape, securely attach a piece of paper (it should be large enough for the wing panel) to the drawing board. Position the T-square firmly against the edge of the drawing board and draw a straight line across the paper; hold your pencil against the blade of the T-square at a constant angle.

Along this line, measure and mark two dots that are the same distance apart as the span of the wing panel. Hold the 60/30 triangle firmly against the blade of the T-square and, at each of these dots, make a vertical line that's the same length as, or slightly longer than, the chord of the wing. Hold the pencil the same as when drawing along the blade of the T-square.

On the rib, measure the distance from the trailing edge to both sides of the main-spar notch, and transfer these measurements to the two vertical lines just drawn. Slide the blade of the T-square up to these

A basic, pencil-drawn plan, with accurate spar and rib locations, is all that's necessary to produce true wing structures.

Full-scale aircraft are built in jigs. In model construction, the plan IS the jig!

marks, keeping the guide firmly against the side of the drawing board, and draw in the spar location. Measure and draw the leading edge in the same way.

Move the T-square below the trailing-edge marks, and use the 60/30 triangle to draw the rib locations, properly spaced, between the leading and trailing edges. Generally, the rib spacing on R/C airplanes will vary with the size of the wing: 2 inches is common for spans up to 50 inches, and $2^1/_2$ inches for spans of 51 to 72 inches or so (assuming aspect ratios of 6 to 1). The plan is now ready to be used as a building jig.

If you follow these guidelines, you'll find that drawing an accurate plan is an easy—and enjoyable—procedure. ■

How to pick a suitable first plane

When you're ready to learn, you'll need a trainer that's a good match for your experience, finances and available time. I'll outline some things you should consider and give you a list of choices.

Almost without exception, a trainer is a high-wing, light airplane with an ample wing. Because of their inherent stability, 3-channel (for rudder, elevator and throttle) planes seem to be the best. They rely on dihedral (the upward slant of the wings toward the tips) to bank the airplane when rudder control is given, and this dihedral adds stability, i.e., it helps the airplane recover to a normal flight path from abnormal attitudes.

To remain in the air, heavy airplanes must fly faster than their lighter counterparts, and this extra speed gives a student much less thinking time in which to react to flight situations. Some of the lightly loaded, lower-powered airplanes (indicated with an * in the lists that follow) could be used as trainers without an instructor. Under no circumstances should you attempt to fly any of the other kits listed without a qualified instructor.

Kits are listed with the least expensive, usually lower-powered, airplanes at the top, followed by the larger, more expensive types. The lists don't include all training airplanes, but only those with which I have experience. ■

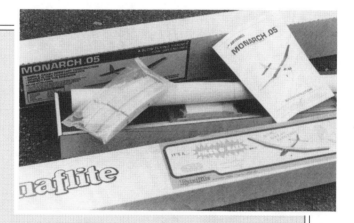

Two of the best—Piece O' Cake and Monarch .05. The kits in list "A" come with excellent instructions that take a lot of the risk out of model building.

LIST A

Trainer Kits

Dynaflite Piece O'Cake *
  2- to 3-channel
  .049-powered
Dynaflite Butterfly*
  3-channel
  .15-powered
Sig Seniorita
  3- to 4-channel
  .15- to .20-powered
Midwest Aero-Sport .20
  4-channel
  .20-powered
Great Planes PT 20
  3-channel
  .20- to .25-powered
Sig Kadet Mark II
  3- to 4-channel
  .25- to .40-powered
Carl Goldberg Eaglet
  3- to 4-channel
  .20- to .25-powered
Goldberg Falcon 56 Mark II
  3- to 4-channel
  .25- to .40-powered
Midwest Aero-Sport .40
  4-channel
  .40-powered

If you have model building experience with free-flight or U-control airplanes, thoroughly enjoy building and feel comfortable with a razor knife and sandpaper, your choice of training airplane is almost unlimited. A few are listed under "A" in my list of trainers. The instructions with most of these kits are so good that prior modeling experience isn't really necessary; you just need the desire and the ability to follow instructions and use simple hand tools.

A few of the trainer kits at the Hobby Counter (Johnny Clemens' famous shop) give an idea of the number and types available.

LIST B

Mostly Prefabricated

Duracraft DuraPlane
   3- to 4-channel
   .20- to .25-powered
Hobbico Sturdy Birdy
   3- to 4-channel
   .25-powered
RPM Models Snark 20T
   3- to 4-channel
   .20-powered
Carl Goldberg Vector
   3- to 4-channel
   .40-powered
Lanier Transit
   3- to 4-channel
   .40-powered

If you can only faintly remember the last balsa (or plastic) model airplane you assembled, but you have some free time and would like to give it another try, the kits listed under "B" are just right. They aren't difficult to build, as they're mostly prefabricated. They're also a good way to introduce someone to the hobby of building, as well as the sport of flying R/C airplanes. (Some of the airplanes in this list have considerably more prefabrication than others and are naturally more expensive, so choose the kit by the time and the funds available.)

This isn't a crash—it's the way almost-ready-to-fly airplanes leave the box! Assembly and installation of engine and radio are "sugar-coated" modeling. ARFs aren't the best trainers, but they'll fill the bill if competent instruction is available.

LIST C

Ready to Fly

Cox RC EZ Bee*
   2- to 3- channel
   .049-powered
MRC Trainer Hawk
   3- to 4- channel
   .20- to .25-powered

There just aren't that many airplanes in this category that qualify as trainers. The Hawk is on the heavy side and not ideal, but you could use it as a trainer under the proper conditions and with the help of a competent instructor. The EZ Bee is sometimes considered to be in the "toy" class, but if properly treated and maintained, it makes a good, inexpensive trainer. These are as close to "ready-to-fly" as you'll find.

The choices are complicated and the pitfalls many. Exercise your best judgment after seeking advice from several sources, including active fliers, R/C club officers and hobby shop operators.

An explanation of the terms you'll hear

There are Federal laws that govern the radio equipment we use to control our airplanes. The most important recent change in the Federal rules is the closer s pacing of R/C channels. Terms like narrow bandwidth, dual conversion, side bands and harmonics are used in connection with these rules and in advertising for the different systems, so it seems appropriate to know just what these terms mean.

Bandwidth

Bandwidth can be applied to both transmitters and receivers. In a transmitter, it's the amount of the frequency spectrum the transmitted signal occupies. In theory, if no information is placed on a signal, it occupies only one precise spot in the spectrum—let's say 72.150MHz. When information is added (modulation), the bandwidth of the signal expands to carry that information. For example, a 1,000-cycle tone would expand the signal 1,000 cycles both above and below the center frequency. Now, the frequency of the transmitted signal is from 72.149 to 72.151MHz.

The more information placed on the signal, the more bandwidth it uses. For example, if a 3,000-cycle tone was also added to the signal, the bandwidth would increase to occupy a space 6KHz wide from 72.147 to 72.153MHz as both tones were transmitted. To accommodate the highest tone transmitter, the bandwidth of the transmitter would be 6KHz. These numbers apply to both AM and narrow-band FM types of modulation.

The receiver that "hears" this transmitted signal must have a bandwidth that's wide enough (in the case of receivers, it's called "passband") to pass the 6KHz of information on the transmitted signal.

It's obvious that the perfect system would be a transmitter that transmitted exactly the width of signal necessary, and the receiver would have a passband exactly wide enough to pass the information from the transmitter. Neither exists!

When an electric current is started or broken, it tends to cause a spark. This resembles what happens to a radio signal when the modulation turns the signal off for an instant, but instead of a spark, ripples of the modulating frequency move out from the center of the transmitted frequency like a rock thrown into water. These spurious signals, or sidebands, cause the transmitted signals to be wider than necessary, and if they're too wide, they can "splatter" into adjacent channels and cause interference. The practical solution is to impose just enough modulation on the signal to make it easily understood by the intended receiver; but not so much that it causes interference to receivers tuned to other channels.

The Receiver

All our receivers are of the superheterodyne type; this is the name applied to a system that converts the incoming signal to a much lower frequency before it's amplified and finally detected. Why is that done? Well, one of the characteristics of a tuned circuit is that the lower the frequency to which it's tuned, the narrower the band of frequencies it will pass (notice the term "band" of frequencies), and the higher the frequency, the wider the band. The superheterodyne receiver was quite an industrial secret in the '20s, and they were sealed in metal boxes so folks wouldn't see what was inside.

The incoming signal is combined (hetrodyned) with a signal generated in the receiver itself. When this happens, two more signals that are the same as the incoming one appear in the mixer stage of the receiver. For example: 72.150MHz (our transmitter frequency) is hetrodyned with a signal of 71.600MHz (in the receiver); frequencies of 143.750MHz (71.60+72.15) and .550MHz (72.15-71.60) are produced.

A number of circuits are tuned to the .550MHz signal, which is much lower, so this makes the circuits much sharper! The 143MHz is tuned out by these same circuits. The .550MHz signal is called the "intermediate frequency" or "IF," and it's amplified and detected to recover the intelligence placed on the original signal by the transmitter.

The receiver could respond to an incoming signal that is .550MHz below the 71.60MHz frequency generated in the receiver, but tuned circuits in stages preceding the mixer should eliminate this so-called image frequency. To increase selectivity, dual-conversion receivers were designed to eliminate any problem from image frequencies when using an "IF" lower than the standard .550MHz.

One problem keeps the received passband from being too sharp. It's called "drift"! Heat and cold affect the transmitter and receiver crystals to the extent that they can drift so far apart that the receiver no longer responds to the transmitter.

The term "narrow band" in front of FM (NBFM) does not mean that the transmitted FM signal is any more narrow than an AM signal. It simply means that it's narrower than a regular FM signal. Both NBFM and AM signals occupy exactly the same amount of the radio spectrum if they both carry the same information.

Over-Modulation

Over-modulation is a condition within the transmitter where the information fed to the radio signal is too strong and will interfere with adjacent channels. Over-modulation of an NBFM signal causes much more interference than the same situation on an AM signal. Both conditions are easily corrected by a qualified technician. Don't throw that old transmitter away; have it checked and any modulation problems solved.

One of the photos shows three of the four pilots who are engaged in a pylon race. They were never more than 10 feet apart, and at no time were they bothered by any form of third-order modulation during this heat or any of the hundreds of heats witnessed in the last 10 years.

Third-order modulation (3IM) interference is the saturation of the first stage of a receiver by a strong signal. Years ago, when radio receivers were crystal sets and two strong signals could be heard at the same time, it was called "cross-modulation." Later, with the advent of vacuum tubes for receivers, the problem almost disappeared, except occasionally, when very near a powerful broadcasting

What are these guys looking at anyway? Must be flying the same plane!

station. By then, it was called "front-end overload," which correctly described the condition.

When transistors came on the scene, strong signals would turn them into crystal detectors and, once again, hearing two stations at the same time was a problem. Just as today, proper receiver design was the solution then. Someone is pulling your leg if they tell you that this 3IM stuff is transmitted and that you should get away from the other pilot! ■

Message received and understood?

The heart of the system—the receiver—pumps information to the servos. Actually, the receiver doesn't tell the servos anything; the decoder takes care of that, but they're both in the same little box, so I'll treat them as one.

The reception of radio signals isn't at all complicated; if your transmitter were very powerful and the only source of radio signals in the world, you could fly your airplane with a receiver that contained only three things:

- *an antenna*
- *a small, tightly wound coil of wire (RF choke)*
- *a diode*

The decoder would still be rather complicated, but the receiver itself would be simple

The receiver is below and the decoder is upside-down on top of it. This piece of equipment is called "a brick." The receiver, decoder and servos were contained in one package; the two servos are on the right. Using all discrete components, the decoder is larger than current IC types.

and very inexpensive!

Unfortunately, in reality, your receiver requires more parts to do its job—receiving only your signal—correctly.

If a receiver is to receive only one signal at any time it must be selective, and this selectivity is acquired by substituting a tuned circuit for the RF choke in the receiver I just described. A single tuned circuit just won't have a sufficiently sharp reception, so you add another. Also, because your transmitter isn't powerful, you need to add some amplification.

After adding many tuned circuits and amplifiers, you still find that your receiver isn't sharp enough.

Selectivity is a function of frequency: the higher the frequency, the broader the response of a tuned circuit, and we operate on what's considered very high frequency in the 70- to 75MHz range. (MHz stands for millions of cycles per second.) Compare that with the standard AM broadcast band, which is given in thousands of cycles per second.

If there were some way in which the 75MHz signal could be brought down to a much lower frequency, our tuned circuits would work very much better. Fortunately, there is a way, and it's called "hetrodyning." To hetrodyne a signal down in frequency, it's mixed with another signal, and the difference between the two is then run through tuned circuits that bring about the selectivity we need. To bring about this magic, another signal is needed—usually about 450kHz (thousand cycles) above or below our received signal—and we also need a device called a "mixer."

A mixer accepts an external signal and one that's generated locally in the receiver. The mixer is followed by a circuit tuned to the difference frequency—about 450kHz. This new frequency is then amplified and sent to our diode detector. The crystal in our receivers governs the frequency of this internal signal—called a local oscillator. The little square metal cans on the receiver board are the circuits that are tuned to the new 450kHz signal.

Because of the local oscillator in your receiver, like your transmitter, it will generate a radio-frequency signal! If you happen to fly close (within 1 foot) to someone whose receiver is tuned to your receiver's crystal frequency (very unlikely!), he will experience radio failure!

Further, since mixers resemble the first amplification stage in our receivers, it's quite possible that our neighbor's transmitted signal, on a different frequency, can mix with ours in the front end of our receiver (this happens!) and then we experience radio failure! This type of mixing can occur in the first stage of various frequency-measuring instruments and give false readings that confuse even the experts operating the equipment. Hetrodynes are a two-edged sword!

After our signal suffers through all the stages necessary to reach the detector, it still has to go to the decoder. This nifty device counts the number, timing and spacing of the pulses that our transmitter encodes on the signal, converts them into information the various servos can understand, and directs the information to the proper servo or servos. If the receiver is the heart, the decoder is the nervous system.

Always remember that heat and cold affect crystal frequency. The pass band (the range of frequencies passed by our receivers) can't be too narrow, or the crystal frequency can change enough to miss our receiver completely! Also consider that, in the very-high-frequency ranges, narrow-band FM transmission isn't one of our most efficient methods of communication.

For additional reading on this subject, I recommend any recent edition of the "ARRL Radio Amateur Handbook." ∎

This picture shows most of the components in a typical modern receiver. The square metal boxes with the central screwdriver slot are shielded coils, tuned to the intermediate frequency (see text). The two coils at the lower right are tuned to the incoming signal. Notice the frequency listed on top of the crystal—52.745M; add that to the IF frequency of .455 MH and you get 53.2MH, which is the signal frequency. The decoder board in this picture uses integrated circuits (ICs) and will operate up to eight servos. The ICs are the things that look like centipedes!

It isn't as difficult as you might think

Let's look at the nuts and bolts of receivers—actually, they're coils, condensers, resistors, diodes, RF chokes, transistors and integrated circuits. An integrated circuit (IC) is just more condensers and resistors, along with some diodes and transistors that have been reduced in size and put into a small package.

The best way to learn about a device is to take it apart and see what makes it tick. Fortunately for us, the people at Ace R/C have already dismantled a very good receiver just so that we can reassemble it! When it has been put back together, it's not only a very good receiver, but it's also inexpensive!

There's little difference between the way manufacturers assemble receivers and the way you and I assemble one on the kitchen table. The trick is knowing where each part goes. In the Ace kit, the assembly manual is our textbook and the diagram of the printed-circuit (PC) board is the plan.

As with any kit, you must first become familiar with the parts. The manual shows them and describes the way in which each is identified. The parts in our radios are no different from those used in any radio, TV or computer, so when you know them, you'll be able to spot them in other applications.

The PC board is drilled to receive the correct part in the right place. Identify the parts, then, following the layout, push the wires through the holes in the top of the board, and solder them to the foil pattern on the bottom.

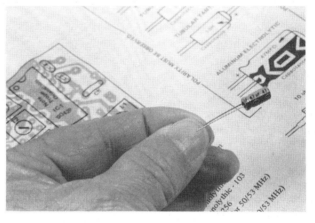

Above: Identifying parts is the first step in building any kit. This is an aluminum electrolytic condenser because the caption under the picture in the manual says so!

Above: Parts are put into the correct place on the top side of the circuit board and...

Right: ...soldered to the foil on the bottom side. A soldering iron with a small tip is a necessary tool for electronic kit building.

Do this a few parts at a time, and solder them, then add a few more, etc. They should be soldered to the foil before the extra lead lengths are removed.

Once all the parts are on the board, the receiver must be aligned. Here, "aligned" means that the receiver must be tuned to your transmitter just as a radio or TV is tuned to a broadcast station. In each of the shielded coils is a threaded slug that can be adjusted to bring the coil into tune. It isn't a difficult procedure, but you must have a tuning wand, which is a little plastic screwdriver, and a good voltmeter or oscilloscope. Alternatively, you can take the receiver, the manual and your transmitter to your local repair shop and have the job done quickly. (Don't forget to take a battery pack as well!)

The receiver shown in the photographs was modified to be used with Kraft servos by installing a Kraft terminal block on the board. Terminal blocks (or connectors) to fit most other servos can be ordered from Ace R/C, along with the receiver kit.

For a small investment in time and money, you can discover a great deal about radios and get a state-of-the-art receiver as part of the bargain. Why not try it! ■

Top: Resistors are usually installed upright because they take up less room that way. One lead is bent parallel to the other and both are slipped into the proper holes in the circuit board.

Bottom: The long leads are cut even with the bottom of the circuit board after they have been soldered to the foil.

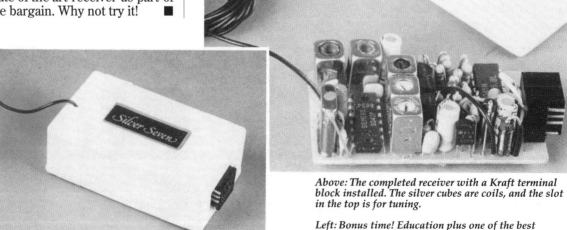

Above: The completed receiver with a Kraft terminal block installed. The silver cubes are coils, and the slot in the top is for tuning.

Left: Bonus time! Education plus one of the best state-of-the-art receivers available.

11 TRANSMITTERS

Our planes obviously don't have pilots aboard, but they do have alternatives—a transmitter and receiver.

A long time ago, it was noted that when the frequency of alternating current (AC) was increased, a point was reached at which some of it left the wire and was radiated into the air; radio had been discovered! In radio, "frequency" means the number of times that a current flow changes direction, or alternates, in 1 second. In the U.S., AC domestic current changes direction 60 times a second and is called "60 cycle."

Radio frequencies begin just above the frequency we're able to hear, i.e., about 15,000 cycles per second, or 15 kilohertz (kHz). When referring to radio, "kilo" means thousands and "hertz" means "cycles per second." Along the same line, "mega" means million, so "megahertz" (MHz) stands for "millions of cycles per second." The standard AM broadcast band extends from 550kHz (thousands) to 1600kHz, or 1.6MHz (millions).

In the beginning, radio waves were generated by a spinning, saw-toothed wheel that was brushed by a wiper. By connecting the wheel to one terminal of a battery and the wiper to the other, every tooth-wiper contact caused a spark! The speed of rotation determined the frequency of the spark that jumped between the contacts. These spark transmitters were noisy; the spark generated radio waves all along the radio frequency (RF) spectrum; and they were quite inefficient; but such transmitters, and simple diode receivers, were actually able to send messages across oceans! But the invention of the vacuum tube quickly spelled their doom.

The Vacuum Tube

The vacuum tube not only made the reception of radio signals better by offering a way to amplify them, but it also made it possible to generate radio waves with a circuit called an "oscillator." This circuit fed some of the amplified signal back into the tube, thus generating a sustained oscillation—like a dog chasing its tail!—which was maintained as long as a voltage was applied to the tube. It was then possible to generate "clean" frequencies into the MH range and higher.

The transistor with which we're all familiar has replaced the vacuum tube in almost all low- and medium-power applications. It can produce the same results with less power input than vacuum tubes,

Above: The part of the transmitter that generates the radio frequency (RF) signal is always close to the antenna. The RF board can be found by the presence of the crystal (the can just to the left of the stick yoke in this picture). Components have changed over the years, but RF is generated in almost the same way as it was 60 years ago, only then it was with vacuum tubes rather than transistors.

Right: The encoder board changes the movement of the control sticks to a series of impulses that are then added to the RF signal by a process called "modulation." The strength of the signal can be varied (AM), or the frequency can be varied (FM) by these impulses. The black buttons with the white centers are throw adjustments for each channel.

and it can do it in a much smaller space. But transistors and their close relative, the integrated circuit, work in almost the same way as vacuum tubes. In other words, our transmitters use the same basic circuits that were used more than 60 years ago!

Crystals

Then, as now, frequency was determined by a mechanical device called a "crystal." When a small electric current is passed through a quartz crystal, it will vibrate at a rate that's dependent on its size

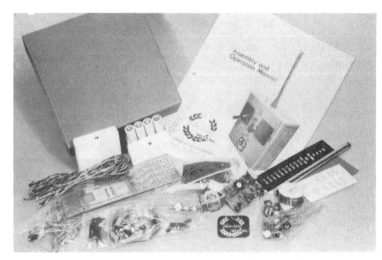

Above: This transmitter kit from Ace R/C has the RF section already wired. The board with its crystal can be seen just below the bottom corner of the transmitter picture on the manual. Kits provide the equipment and the chance to to learn about it.

Left: This transmitter is more than 15 years old, and the signal is still clean and right on frequency! Regular maintenance and care, battery changes and common sense will allow equipment to function for hundreds of hours, as in this case.

Below: The last of the American-made transmitters by Kraft. This one is a dandy! Metal boxes help to eliminate the effects of our hands on the electronics inside, and they're well worth the additional cost. It's the transmitter that puts you in the cockpit; get good ones and treat them kindly!

and thickness. Thus, by grinding them to a specific size, crystals can be used to set the frequency of an oscillator. Crystals are used to control the frequency of our transmitters, and they're used to keep our receivers stable.

Crystals aren't a panacea for frequency instability, because they change according to temperature. For this reason, compensatory circuits are usually included in our transmitters and receivers, but they only alleviate, and don't eliminate the problem! Don't leave your transmitter in the sun!

Modulation

When the radio frequency is generated by the oscillator, if it's to be of any use, a message must be put on the signal. In the beginning, it was enough to turn the transmitter on and off to send messages and, later, to control the rudder in our R/C airplanes, but now we have to send much more information to the receiver than a simple yes or no. A process called "modulation" is used to put information into the radio signal. The movements of the sticks and trims are translated into pulses by an encoder, then superimposed on the RF signal by the modulator.

In our transmitters, this modulation is accomplished in two ways:
—the frequency is changed slightly (FM), or
—the strength or amplitude (AM) of the signal is changed.

FM is a little less expensive to generate because it can be introduced into lower levels of the transmitter. AM requires more modulating power because it's introduced into later—or "output"—stages. In practice, given the same bandwidth, the AM signal is the better of the two. Some time in the future, when a computer-generated and -detected type of transmission (pocket radio) is developed for R/C, the type of modulation used will be of no importance.

Single-Stick Transmitters

Look at the photograph that shows Joe Wagner's interesting modification to a single-stick transmitter. Single-stick transmitters invariably have the throttle control on the right side of the transmitter, and you have to cradle the transmitter on the palm and wrist of your left hand so that your fingers can control the throttle lever. This is

This transmitter has been customized to fit a specific need—maybe yours!

an unnatural position for a right-handed person, and it's almost impossible for someone who's left-handed. Many have mastered this system, but it has never been popular.

That extra lever and knob on Joe's transmitter is the throttle. By shifting the elevator trim to the opposite side and using the slot left vacant for the throttle, the transmitter is made operable from a tray, or by someone who is left-handed. The throttle pot must be relocated to the left of the stick. A simple right-angle bracket can be used to mount it in the new position. The new, longer throttle arm is attached to the old arm and is routed through the trim slot, then bent to a convenient position.

The throttle so arranged can be reached easily by fingers of the same hand that operates the stick. The other hand is now free to hold the transmitter any way the flier feels comfortable. This modification will be different for various makes of transmitters, but the principle remains the same. Transmitters so modified may well be

the answer for left-handed modelers who have trouble adapting to standard Mode II transmitters.

Our transmitters are made to be used, and the more we use them, the better and more smoothly the sticks will pass their messages to the encoder and on to the receiver. Don't neglect your transmitter; keep it clean, charged, and away from sun, dust and rain, and it will give years of service. ∎

Some information to help you choose

A simple sheet mock-up to demonstrate control operation (see text).

Much has been written about the changes that will be made to our R/C channels and systems in 1991. Some of this information is not only confusing, but also misleading! Since all radio equipment must eventually be replaced or updated, some basic advice about buying equipment is in order. The R/C system is actually the least expensive part of the airplane, and if you follow my advice, you'll avoid some common problems.

A 100-percent-perfect system just doesn't exist; even in the most ideal situations, operating problems and failures occur, but the more care you take when choosing and operating a system, the fewer will be your problems.

Choosing an R/C System

The Receiver

● Check with local fliers, R/C clubs and hobby shops to find out which channels must be avoided in your area. Our channels mix with much more powerful commercial radio services, and this can render certain channels useless. Which channels are affected varies by area, so local information is vital.

In each AMA district, there's supposed to be a Frequency Coordinator who keeps track of this sort of thing, but his information is only as good as that which he receives from local fliers. It's easier to start with equipment on a clear channel rather than to be subjected to the inconvenience and expense of changing later!

● Don't buy or use equipment on channels 12 and 56! Without going into a long explanation, channel 12 can cause problems with channel 56. The problems can be partly solved by using a properly designed dual-conversion receiver, but since you can't ensure this, it's best to avoid these channels in the first place!

● Any receiver you buy should have a "double balanced mixer," and if it's one of the dual-conversion types, it should have two! This type of mixer is less affected by overloading, which causes the infamous intermodulation interference we've all heard about.

● AM modulation is just as good as, or better than, any other type, regardless of price, and it's just as "narrow-banded," too. A receiver doesn't have to be highly sensitive; in some cases, it could even be a disadvantage.

● Luxury features like LED displays, exponential rates, channel mixing, etc., add to the enjoyment of flying, but they don't increase a system's reliability, so buy what you like and enjoy—but don't expect to have a safer system just because it cost more!

The Transmitter

Receivers are the important link between us and the airplane, but our choice of transmitter isn't quite as crucial. Most available transmitters do a pretty good job In the photograph, you'll see a mock-up of a control system that was used to demonstrate the importance of frequency control. Several transmitter/receiver systems were operated on the same frequency to show how interference affects our ability to control an R/C aircraft. Regardless of the type of modulation used—AM, FM, or PM (Phase Modulation)—the results were the same. When any other signal appeared on the same frequency, there was complete loss of control.

The device is built from sheet balsa with masking-tape hinges. The two servos are mounted with double-sided tape, and the pushrods are music wire with Z-bends in each end. Various receivers are connected to the servos with patch cords that match the connections on the receivers to those of the servos.

The demonstration is impressive, and when it's done at club meetings, it usually improves the use of the frequency-control systems at the flying field. Everyone tends to take things for granted, so an occasional gentle reminder is necessary to remind us of the things we've become too casual about. It would be great if every newcomer to our sport could see such a demonstration and hear the explanation of how the frequency-control system works at his field. When you're flying R/C aircraft, you have a responsibility to other fliers. ■

These control your airplane's movements

The term "servo" is short for "servo-mechanism"—an "electronic system in which a controlling mechanism is actuated by a low-energy signal." The servo is the "controlling mechanism" in an R/C system. The receiver receives the signal from the transmitter and, through a decoder, it tells the servo how to move.

Each aircraft control surface, or function, usually has its own servo to direct its movement, and each servo requires a separate signal, or channel, for proper operation. If the receiver is the "heart" of the system, the servo is the "muscle." A basic "full-house" system (four channels) would have four servos to control:

- elevator
- rudder
- ailerons
- engine throttle.

Internally, each servo is the same and operates similarly. The receiver's job is partly to sort through the received signals and tell each servo how to act. Since all servos are the same, the place at which they're plugged into the receiver will dictate their function.

Although there are slight variations between servos produced by different manufacturers, servos always contain:
- a small circuit board
- a small electric motor
- a variable resistor (like the volume control on your stereo) that's connected through a gear train to the motor and the output arm.

Almost without exception, servos from different manufacturers are interchangeable if their plugs are rewired to conform to the receiver sockets.

In very simple terms: when the servo receives a signal, it causes an imbalance in the circuit, the motor starts to run (its direction will depend on the imbalance) and it continues to run until the movement of the variable resistor through the gear chain brings the circuit back into balance. Since the output arm is attached to the same shaft as the variable resistor, it follows this movement. A small imbalance causes a small movement, and a large imbalance causes a large movement, hence, proportional control of the output arm depends on the amount of movement sent to the servo through movements of the transmitter stick.

Now that we have some idea of how servos

Servos in three sizes demonstrate the different types of output arms. Because they come from different manufacturers, they plug into different types of sockets on the various receivers. There's little standardization in the R/C hobby!

work, let's look at how they should be connected to the control system of an airplane.

As a rule, the output arm of most servos has a circular movement through about 90 degrees, or so—45 degrees in each direction. As long as we stay in the same plane as the arm, we can therefore always depend on a pushing or pulling movement from it. In the airplane, the servos can be mounted parallel to the fuselage or across it; upside-down or right-side-up; they'll always give us the same movement. This is quite convenient, because in most installations, the servos are mounted lengthwise, crosswise and upside-down!

Consider two, different, 4-channel airplanes: a low-wing type and a high-wing type. In the high-wing airplane, the throttle servo, the elevator servo and the rudder servo are mounted in the fuselage cabin area and are usually upright with respect to the airplane. The aileron servo is mounted at the center of the wing and is upside-down (if it were right-side-up, it would have to be on the outside of the airplane to work properly!). Conversely, in the low-wing airplane, the throttle, elevator and rudder servos are upside-down and the aileron servo in the wing is right-side-up. The throttle servo is mounted across the fuselage to provide a little more room in the cabin area in front of the servos.

Servos are best mounted in a plastic or wooden tray that's mounted in the airplane. The rubber grommets in the servos' mounting holes help to dampen the effects of vibration. For this reason, the screws holding the servos to the tray should be tightened only just enough to hold the servos securely without crushing the grommets.

The laden servo tray is one of the radio system's heaviest components, and it should be able to slide forward or backward on mounting rails along each side of the fuselage so that the airplane can be properly balanced when the batteries and receiver are put into place. When the best location for the tray has been determined, it should be secured in that position; and the pushrods to the elevator, rudder and throttle should be connected to the appropriate servos.

The servo that controls the ailerons is mounted at the wing's center section. The usual strip aileron installation uses both sides of the servo output arm; two pushrods and two control horns (one for each aileron) are used to give the required opposite movements to these surfaces.

Servos are subjected to much abuse during a flying season

(especially those that control the rudder and some form of ground steering wheel at the same time), so check them carefully before every flight. Servos should respond quickly to the transmitter's command, and they shouldn't have any "dead" spots along their travel. If you have a servo that jitters or seems to "hunt," you can usually correct it by having the gear train and the variable resistor (or "pot")

thoroughly cleaned by a service technician.

If, as I said at the beginning, the servos are the "muscles" of the radio system, you now know how to keep them pumping! ∎

Left: Building a servo from a kit (this is from Ace R/C) is relatively inexpensive and is one of the best ways to become familiar with a most important part of our control systems. Knowledge is power!

Above: The inside of a typical servo. When the servo receives a signal, the motor drives the output arm through a series of gears (white) as well as a variable resistor (screw-mounted just above the electronics). Like a volume control on a radio, the variable resistor limits the movement to the instructions encoded on the signal.

Some definitions and tips on care

A while ago, I heard from someone who was having problems with a plane I designed. The first part of each flight was as it should be, but when it started mild aerobatics, its control response changed, and that led to the end of flying for the day. He followed a variety of suggestions, but just couldn't find and correct the source of this erratic behavior.

Eventually, after suffering a complete loss of control, he discovered that the cold winter weather was reducing the output voltage of his dry-cell battery pack to a non-functioning level! Checking the battery voltage indoors before and after flying sessions hadn't revealed the problem, but he soon solved it by changing to a Ni-Cd battery pack. Incidentally, the terms "battery" and "cell" aren't interchangeable: a battery is made up of two or more cells.

Many manufacturers ship their radio systems with dry-cell batteries as the source of transmitter and receiver power. It enables them to reduce their costs and produce a less expensive product for a very competitive market. Dry cells differ from Ni-Cd cells in more ways than their inability to be re-charged, and these differences are important.

Dry cells have a nominal voltage rating of 1.5 volts, whereas Ni-Cds are rated at 1.2 volts. This seems to indicate that three dry cells would provide almost as much voltage as four Ni-Cds, (4.5 volts versus 4.8 volts) but this isn't always true. The internal resistance of a cell limits its ability to supply a large current output without suffering a voltage drop. Dry cells have a higher internal resistance than Ni-Cd cells. This means that under high current demand, like that drawn by a servo in operation against a load, they can show a voltage drop and, near the end of their useful life, this drop could cause equipment failure. You can, however, take precautions that will help them to be reliable during their usable life.

Alkaline Cells

Alkaline cells are the only type of dry cell worthy of consideration. A new set in a flight pack for a 2- or 3-channel system should give about 5 or 6 hours of dependable flight time before it has to be replaced. The trick is knowing when their time is up, and there's only one sure way to do this: keep an accurate log of all on time and don't cheat on the replacement time. Granted, new cells would run a flashlight

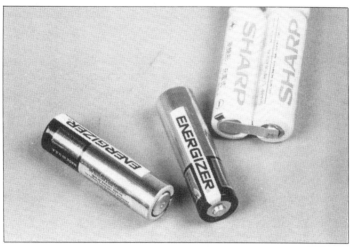

Two sources of power—dry cells and Ni-Cds. With proper care, dry cells will work well in our R/C equipment, but "proper care" is the key.

longer than 5 1/2 hours, and they should run a radio system longer, too, but a flashlight costs a lot less than an airplane and wouldn't be damaged (or injure someone) if one cell fails!

Battery Care

After every flying session, remove the cells from the battery box, then clean and polish their terminals and the battery box terminals with a paper towel or a cloth. When the box terminals are difficult to reach, clean them with the eraser on the end of a pencil.

Check the tension of the battery-box terminals to ensure that good, vibration-proof contact is made with each cell. The battery box in your airplane should be protected from vibration with foam or other vibration-reducing material. In addition, dry-cell battery boxes aren't recommended for airplanes powered by large engines.

You can check your battery with a voltmeter. The battery must be working when you check it, because simply checking a cell without a load can give a very wrong impression of its ability. As well as this, alkaline cells are designed to deliver their rated 1.5 volts until they're exhausted—they shouldn't show a voltage drop.

The cells that make up the transmitter battery should last longer than those in the flight pack, but they should still be replaced every other time the flight pack is replaced. This is especially true if the transmitter doesn't have a visible voltmeter. Dry-cell battery packs may be inexpensive for manufacturers, but they aren't inexpensive for modelers; each time the transmitter and receiver packs are replaced, the cost represents quite an investment, even at discount store "bargain" prices.

Rechargeable Ni-Cds

By far the least expensive, most reliable, way to power your system is by using rechargeable Ni-Cd batteries in your transmitter and flight packs. Ni-Cd packs and inexpensive chargers are readily available.

Available in most hobby shops, the reliable Nobel switch and Deans connectors represent the best offered by the industry for connecting a flight battery to existing systems. The use of department-store Ni-Cds as replacements for alkaline cells in battery boxes is definitely not recommended. Only Ni-Cd cells with solder tabs should be used, and all connections to the cells, switch and connectors must be soldered correctly.

Alkaline cells will provide the power for our systems, but if we want them to be dependable, they must be treated with respect and given the proper care. That's a battery basic! ■

It would be difficult to run any household without a hammer, a screwdriver and pliers, but it's nearly impossible to build model airplanes without the appropriate tools!

Razor knife: The first tool you should buy is a razor knife. Although a single-edge razor blade can be used instead of a razor knife, it's better to consider the razor blade as an addition to your tool kit rather than as a substitute. There are many brands and types of razor-knife handles; just pick one that's comfortable and easy to use.

The most popular and useful blade for any handle is the no. 11—a triangular-shaped blade with a sharp point. When the blade becomes dull, discard it

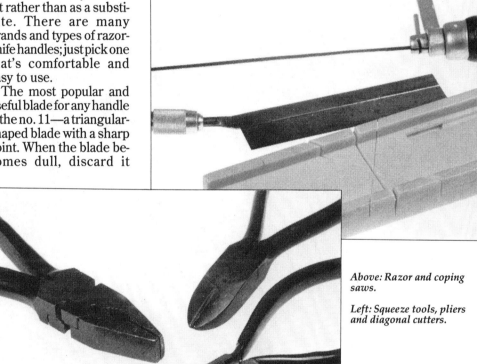

Above: Razor and coping saws.

Left: Squeeze tools, pliers and diagonal cutters.

(carefully!) and insert another into the handle. Dull knives are much more dangerous than sharp ones because of the extra pressure needed to make them cut—and cut badly, at that!

Razor saws and jigsaws: A razor knife is the primary cutting tool, but razor saws and jigsaws are also very useful Used with a miter box, the razor saw is very handy for making straight, smooth cross-cuts in balsa strips to produce good, solid joints. The angled slot in the box makes fast work of sawing right-angle gussets. The coping saw, or jigsaw, is a must for cutting plywood, or any of the harder woods or dowels.

Hand drill: Although most kits are largely prefabricated, it's unusual for the firewall to be drilled. Because there's a wide variety of engine makes and sizes, kit manufacturers leave the selection of the engine and the mount to you. A hand drill and an assortment of drill bits are almost necessities for installing engine mounts on firewalls and for drilling the mount to accept the engine. The essential drill bits include $1/16$-, $3/32$-, $1/8$-, $5/32$-, $3/16$- and $1/4$-inch sizes. The smallest size is for drilling extra holes in servo arms; the largest is for mounting hardwood dowels.

Screwdrivers: It goes without saying that if engines are mounted with screws, you'll need an assortment of screwdrivers. Both conventional and Phillips-head screws are used in modeling, so screwdrivers are needed for both. Blade widths of $1/4$ and $1/8$ inch will suffice for conventional screws, and Phillips-head drivers with $3/32$- and $1/8$-inch shafts should be adequate. Good tools with hard blades are well worth the extra few cents!

Squeeze tools, pliers and diagonal cutters: These are the heavyweights in a modeler's tool box. A pair of heavy-duty, flat-nose pliers takes a lot of the work out of bending wire for landing gear and wing mounts. (Even with good, heavy pliers, it isn't an easy job!) Diagonal cutters are good for cutting wire up to $3/32$ inch in diameter; for larger wire, use bolt cutters. Heavy wire will ruin a pair of diagonal cutters almost instantly.

Long-nose pliers are great for bending small, soft wire and for holding nuts in place while you're installing screws. These pliers act like long, skinny fingers, and they're useful for fishing dropped items from the small dark, places they seem to like so well! Every modeler should have a pair; those with 2-inch-long jaws seem to be the right size.

Paintbrushes: of various sizes, from $1/8$ to $1/2$ inch (including the throwaway kinds for spreading epoxy). Good-quality brushes, properly cleaned after use, will outlast the cheap ones many times over. When it comes to tools, you usually get what you pay for, and the best is always a bargain!

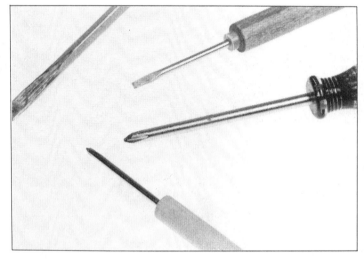

Left: Conventional and Phillips-head screwdrivers.

Below: Hand drill and bits.

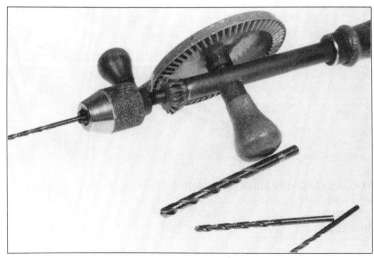

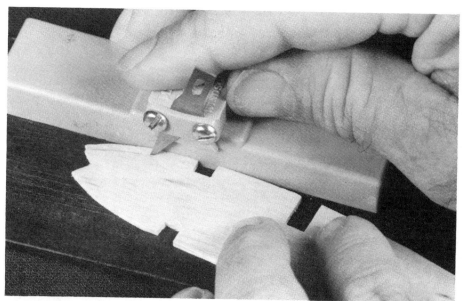

Another use for the balsa stripper.

Steel straight pins complete the basic tool requirements, but there are a number of other tools that have been specially made for modelers, and many modelers make their own tools for specific jobs.

The balsa stripper is very handy and, in the photo, it's being used to trim ribs so that center-section sheeting can lie even with the rest of the ribs. Simply adjust the stripper to the proper width and slice around the rib. This trick has been used by old-timers to taper the last ribs in those elliptical tips that were so popular on airplanes of the "Golden Age" of aviation.

Although not strictly a "tool," no modeler can work without a building board, and your lumber yard is the best source of material for this. Buy a piece of Homosote®.

The basic tools I've listed will help you to accomplish 95 percent of your modeling tasks. Experience with them will give you the skills you'll need to acquire those additional tools that clutter the walls and drawers of all modelers' workshops! ∎

It isn't all the same

MOST R/C airplanes are built from kits, and when you select a kit, you should consider not only the plane's size and appearance, but also the quality of the material used. If you aren't familiar with the materials, it will be impossible for you to judge their quality. Hardware (wire, nuts, bolts, screws, wheels, etc.) isn't difficult to evaluate; but judging balsa is more difficult. Even if balsa is white and clear, it doesn't mean it's suitable for a particular job, and some knowledge of balsa—the most frequently used model-building material—is essential.

Kit materials are usually of a very high quality but, despite the care taken by manufacturers, sub-standard wood sometimes finds its way into kit boxes. If you're knowledgeable about balsa and its characteristics, you can replace a piece of wood with one from your dealer's stock. For just a few cents, you can save yourself future trouble and frustration.

Balsa Basics

Most balsa is grown in Central and South America; some is cultivated, but most is harvested from the wild. Balsa grows quickly and is ready to be harvested in only six to seven years. When it's cut, the wood retains a lot of moisture, which must be removed by kiln or air drying before the wood can be sawn into timber for shipping.

Because of balsa's insulating qualities, the ship-building industry consumes millions of board feet of it each year. This demand generates the high levels of production, which results in the low balsa prices we enjoy.

Balsa is the basic construction material for model airplanes, from the lightest indoor models to the largest giant scale ones. It's unique in that it can be as light as a feather or as strong as pine, and depending on how it's cut, it can be rigid or flexible.

To understand its unique qualities, look at the cross-sectional view of a balsa plank. The curving rings aren't necessarily annual rings, but I'll call them that for the sake of description. The light streaks that go from the center of the rings outward like the spokes of a wheel are the medullary rays. These rays, and the angle at which a sheet of wood is cut to them, give the wood its character.

Broadly speaking, there are three types of sheet balsa. Of course, the actual grain always runs lengthwise to the sheet, so the types are based on the sheet's relationship to the rays.

- "A-grain" is cut with the rays perpendicular to the face of the sheet
- "C-grain" is cut with the rays perpendicular to the edge of the sheet.
- "B-grain" is cut so that the rays intersect the face of the sheet between 40 and 70 degrees.

In the cross-sectional view of the balsa plank, A-grain would be cut from either the right or left side, B-grain from the bottom, and C-grain from the top third. Depending on which face the sheet is sawn from, this plank would produce all three types of grain. In reality, few cut sheets are exactly A-, B-, or C-grain, but they're close enough for our purposes.

Identifying Grains in Sheet Wood

The photo shows the different grains in sheet wood.
- C-grain has a mottled, almost iridescent look.
- B-grain appears to have a grain that runs lengthwise.
- A-grain shows a long, smooth grain that

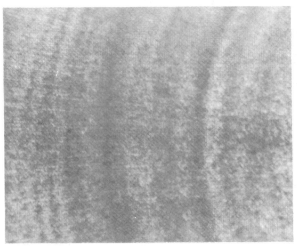

This cross-section of a balsa log shows the annual rings and the medullary rays, which radiate likes spokes of a wheel.

seems to run the entire length of the sheet. Sheets often have a different grain on each side, because one side was sawn from planks closer to the center of the log.

Uses of the Various Grains

A-grain wood is ideal for sheeting curved surfaces because it's quite flexible across the sheet. In fact, thin sheets can be soaked in water and rolled into tubes, and this is how we make tail booms for very light models. C-grain is rather stiff and is very good for ribs and formers because it tends to hold its shape under stress. B-grain is a general-purpose wood that resembles the other two, but isn't as rigid as C-grain or as flexible as A-grain. It makes good fuselage sides, longerons, and spars.

Balsa is available in specific weights of 4 to 15 or more pounds per cubic foot. The lightest is useful for indoor model airplanes, which must be very light; the heaviest balsa has few uses because pine or spruce may be used in its place. For most R/C construction, the ideal weights are in the 5- to 10-pound range. The lightest wood in this range is excellent for solid tail groups and movable surfaces, and the heavier (9- to 10-pound) wood is used for spars and longerons. The mid-range (7- to 8-pound) stock is fine for ribs and fuselage sides, and it's often referred to as "medium" balsa.

When buying 1/16-inch stock for ribs, or any part that must be cut out with a razor knife, hold the wood up to the light and look for a regular and evenly spaced grain. Some sheets contain harder "streaks" that are difficult to cut with a razor knife.

As you read on, you'll find out just which weight and cut of wood is right for a particular job. Kit building is one of the best ways to learn, because manufacturers try to select the correct wood for each part so that they fit into the complete airframe.

Balsa is an easily cut soft wood with which you'll enjoy working. It doesn't take long to become an expert. ∎

Left: Three sheets of 1/16-inch balsa. They look alike, but they're from woods of different weights.

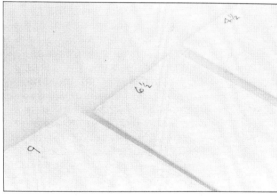

Right: Three sheets of balsa with three different grains. Left to right: C grain, B grain and A grain.

Left: In these balsa sheets, the darker areas are the hardest parts. Evenly spaced grain is usually easier to slice with a razor knife.

For that finishing touch

It has been said that the difference between a craftsman and a hacker is sandpaper. It brings the finishing touch to every project.

"Sandpaper" is actually a misnomer; very little real sandpaper is used in modeling. The paper is usually covered with garnet or aluminum oxide, both of which last much longer than sand, and they don't leave bits of abrasive in the wood, as sand sometimes does. Although aluminum oxide is more expensive, it's well worth the cost. In this book, the terms "sandpaper" or "sanding" will refer to all three types of paper.

Aside from the type of abrasive and its grit size, another piece of information that's printed on the back of sandpaper is whether its coat is "open" or "closed." Closed-coat paper is designed to pick up and hold the sanding dust, so it's of little use to us. Open-coat paper releases the dust so that you can continue to work. Most sandpaper is of the open-coat variety, but check before you buy.

The most obvious difference between sandpapers is in the size of the grit that makes up the abrasive; the larger the number, the finer the grit. Shaping is done with 80, 100 and 150 sizes, and finishing with 320, 400 and 600 sizes. The 400 and 600 sizes usually come in "wet-or-dry" versions, so they can be used to finish painted surfaces as well as wooden ones. When wet, they act as closed-coat paper to give paint a polished finish.

Sanding Blocks

To get the most from sandpaper, it should be backed up with an inflexible material—usually a wooden block. Buy a 1x2 from your local lumber yard, cut it into several 12-inch lengths and wrap them with sandpapers with a variety of grits. This type of block is quite useful for sanding completed structures before you cover them. Use thumb tacks to hold the sandpaper in place on the block.

For sanding inside curves (e.g., gussets or fairings), you can make other types of block by wrapping sandpaper around hardwood dowels of various sizes. For hard-to-reach places, glue a single piece of sandpaper to a thin strip of wood. Make the tool fit the job.

Proper Sanding Procedures

As a rule, all sanding should be done with the grain of the wood, rather than across it. One

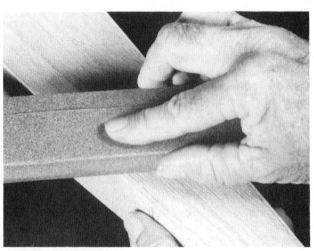

Above: For smoothing sheet-balsa fuselages sides, 100-grit sandpaper wrapped around a 1x2-inch block is ideal. If you're using heat-shrink covering, sand with 320-grit paper before finishing.

Below: A sanding block wrapped with 150-grit paper is the proper tool for smoothing and shaping open structures. Sandpaper of this grit will quickly round edges and corners, so use only very light pressure.

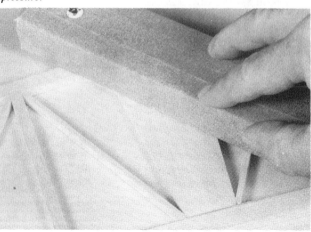

exception is when you're using a sanding block to shape or carve. Cowlings and fairings can be shaped against the grain. After you've achieved the required shape, however, return to the "with-the-grain" rule.

To smooth any glue bumps or other irregularities on the joints of a finished structure, sand first with a block wrapped in 100-grit sandpaper. Next, shape and smooth the fuselage, the leading and trailing edges of the wings and the tail surfaces so that all the edges are rounded.

Use long, smooth strokes, and let the paper do the work. You shouldn't have to apply any pressure other than the weight of the block. Brush or blow any sanding dust away from the work as you go, and occasionally dust the sandpaper with a paintbrush to remove anything that might adhere to the grit. Don't be in a hurry; enjoy the feel of the abrasive cutting and smoothing the wood.

Next, use 150-grit paper and sand in the direction in which air will flow over the surface or part. When sanding the wing, sand from the leading edge to the trailing edge with the sanding block spanwise, so that several ribs are covered at the same time. Again, use long, smooth strokes, and don't be in a hurry. Sanding takes very little time compared with the time spent in construction, and it pays large dividends when the covering or paint is applied.

Finally, slide your fingers all along the structure that will be exposed to the covering and smooth any rough spots with 320-grit paper.

A sanding block isn't limited to sanding finished structures: used in combination with the edge of the workbench, it's a good way to smooth an end or to "edge-on" strip or sheet wood. The edge of

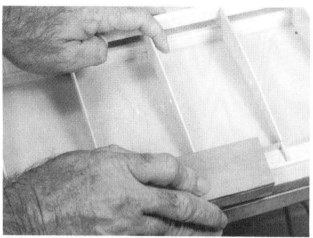

When sanding wings, place the trailing edge at the edge of the bench so that the sanding block can assume the proper angle to blend it into the airfoil. Generally, the sanding stroke should be with the grain of the wood.

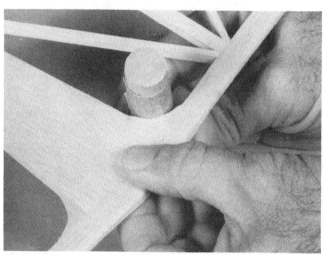

To finish the inside curves of fillets and gussets, use 150-grit sandpaper wrapped around dowels of various sizes.

the bench acts as a sanding guide to keep the face of the block at a fixed angle to the work. When strips are cut with a razor knife, the cut often isn't at the exact angle you need for a tight joint. You can make the correction more quickly and accurately by using the sanding block and the bench edge than by re-cutting the strip with a knife.

The edges of die-cut parts are often slightly crushed or splintered, so you should sand them before you start construction. A sanding block with 150-grit paper is just right for forming the crisp edges that make solid joints. Strips of sandpaper glued to one surface of spar stock can be used to sand the notches in ribs and formers.

Sanding should always be done in a well-ventilated area. A box fan can be used as an exhaust fan by attaching an air conditioner filter to the back of it and doing your sanding on the filter side. This system will control the dust quite well if the filter is changed (or cleaned) when it's dirty. Balsa dust is very light, and it will cover everything in the shop if you let it.

Sanding sealants and fillers are important adjuncts to sandpaper, but for the most part, sport-type airplanes built without them will still look beautiful—but not without sandpaper! ■

Above: Here, sandpaper wrapped around a wire is used to carve notches in the wing's trailing edge so that the aileron arms can work properly and freely. When sandpaper stops cutting, don't apply more pressure— get new paper. The sandpaper should always do the work.

Left: Bond paper can be used as a mask to protect areas that don't need to be sanded (as in this case of blending a wing tip into the airfoil). Without the mask, the spars and ribs would be reduced in height and the airfoil compromised.

Right: Wrap a portion of the sanding block with paper; the effect is similar to that of a mask. Here, the trailing edge of a foam wing is being formed. The paper wrap keeps the sandpaper from cutting into the wood while you're sanding the foam. Use short strokes in this application.

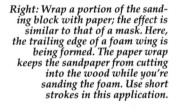

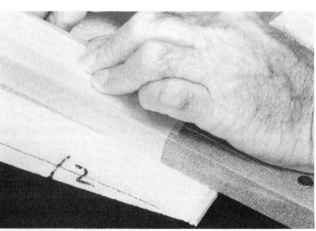

You need the right one for the job

The best materials and wood are of little use to a modeler unless he has some way to join them and, of course, model airplane glue comes immediately to mind.

These glues (or cements) are made with solvents (e.g., acetone) that evaporate quickly, and they rely on this evaporation to cure. Until the advent of the glow engine with its need for an alcohol-based fuel, solvent-based glues were the only ones that were really useful to modelers. Alcohol will dissolve model airplane cement just as well as acetone does.

Even though alcohol fuel is the most prevalent, model airplane cement (e.g., Ambroid and Testors) is still one of the lightest glues, and it will hold well for years. It's excellent for balsa structures that are protected from engine exhaust by paint or plastic covering materials.

To make a good joint with model airplane glue, apply a little glue to the pieces to be joined; let it dry; then add more glue and join. This method gives the wood a chance to absorb some of the glue. Forty-year-old model airplanes that were glued this way are still flying, and this glue definitely has a place in every modeler's workshop.

White and Aliphatic Glues

When it became apparent that glow fuel could dissolve the glue on joints, modelers turned to "hot fuel-proofing." They painted a clear, impervious, fuel-resistant finish over the entire airplane. This practice gave way to finishes and glues that were already fuel-proof: enter the white glues.

White glues, such as Elmers, are generally unaffected by alcohol and are water-resistant. Note that "water-resistant" doesn't mean "waterproof." A waterproof glue joint must withstand boiling for a period of time, and not just a soaking. For a good joint when using white glue, the parts should be clamped together for a time, but for our purposes, white glue can be treated like model airplane cement (no double application). It does, how-

ever, require a longer drying time, and it weighs more.

Aliphatic resin, or yellow glue, is an improvement on the white glues, not only in strength, but in the way it reacts to sanding. White glue tends to ball-up when it's sanded (even after it has cured well), but the aliphatic glues can be sanded very effectively. The white and aliphatic glues don't have to be

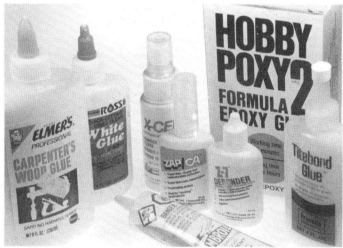

To experienced modelers, these glues are as familiar as the key to the family car, but to the inexperienced, they can be quite confusing. Here are two kinds of aliphatic resin glues (Elmer's Carpenters' and Titebond): model airplane cement (Ambroid): white glue (Ross), and cyanoacrylate, or CA (Zap) with a speed cure (X-Cell) and a debonder (Z-7) for this superfast adhesive.

spread on both surfaces to be joined, but it's a good idea.

These glues work well when you're gluing balsa to balsa and plywood to balsa, e.g., attaching plywood doublers to balsa fuselage sides. If you spread these glues over large areas that are to be joined, the pieces will warp, so you should dampen the opposite sides with water to counteract this warping.

White and aliphatic glues are the best choice for gluing balsa to foam, because they don't attack foam, and most other types do. These glues are also water-based, so they can be cleaned up easily before they cure.

Epoxies and Cyanoacrylates

So far, I've talked about glues that cure in air, but epoxies and cyanoacrylates (CAs) cure by chemical action. Epoxy glues come in two parts that must be mixed together before they can be used. Since those available have different curing times, they can be used for a variety of jobs. Rapid-curing glue works well for field repairs, whereas slow-curing glue is used over large surfaces and for jobs that might require changes in alignment prior to final assembling.

Epoxies were the first quick-curing glues, and they cured in as little as 1 minute, or even less. For general model assembly, the 30- to 60-minute types are the best, and you should mix a new batch when the "old" one starts to thicken.

Epoxies cure more quickly in warm weather, so can speed curing with a heat gun, which thins the glue. Because there's no evaporation or shrinking, epoxies are heavier than other types of glue. Use them for mounting firewalls and in areas where the accumulation of oil or fuel could be a problem.

CAs have revolutionized modeling. These glues (Hot-Stuff, Jet, etc.) can cure instantly or take several minutes, so they can be used in almost any application. These products have reduced drying time to zero!

If you use the thin, instant-curing variety of CA, then the pieces to be joined must be in good contact with one another before the glue is applied and allowed to wick into the joint. For a good bond, solid wood-to-wood joints must be made. Fill gaps with baking soda or sawdust so that the glue will wick into the joint.

The thicker, slower CAs (Super Jet, Super-T, etc.) will fill gaps. In fact, when used with one of the accelerators, fillets can be built up around a joint by alternating glue and accelerator. With the exception of gluing foam, the thick CAs can be used as substitutes for the other glue types. The disadvantages of CAs are that they're heavy when applied too

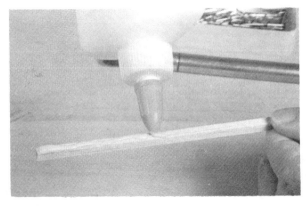

Left: White and aliphatic-resin glues come in bottles that make it easy to open and seal after use. This is a twist-to-close applicator, which can be adjusted to release a precise amount of glue.

Right: The thin CAs are allowed to soak, or "wick," into a joint: here, it's being applied to T-nuts on the rear of a firewall. Thicker CAs can be used in almost the same way as the aliphatic glues, but they have a much, much faster curing time.

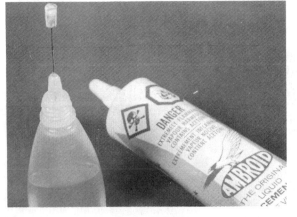

Left: The one that started it all: model airplane cement. A small plastic bottle, a hypodermic needle for a nozzle and a piece of .015 wire for a stopper make a great way to apply model airplane glue that has been thinned with acetone. This arrangement will enable you to put, glue into places that would otherwise be impossible to reach.

thickly, and they cause allergic reactions in some people. They'll bond to human skin almost instantly, so make sure that the glue is put onto the joint and not on your hand. Fortunately, debonders will remove unwanted glue.

You'll soon learn which type of glue suits you, and which is best for a specific job. Some of us enjoy building and are in no hurry for the job to be completed, while others want a finished model as soon as possible. Choose the product that suits you. ■

All those little details!

The hardware packages included in model kits are often incomplete—you must supply the engine mount, fuel tank and wheels. Kit manufacturers aren't necessarily trying to cuts costs, but rather to accommodate the needs of many modelers.

Because inexperienced fliers tend to use smaller engines, while those with more air time want a larger engine's snappier performance, manufacturers design their kits to perform safely with both, and they advertise them as suitable for a range of engine sizes.

Engine Mounts

Different engines require different mounts, and in an airplane kit for .20 to .45 engines, a manufacturer would have to include five or six different mounts. Even two engines in the .20 range can require different mounts, as might a 2- and a 4-stroke engine of the same, or similar, displacement!

Fuel Tanks

Mounts aren't the only thing that changes with

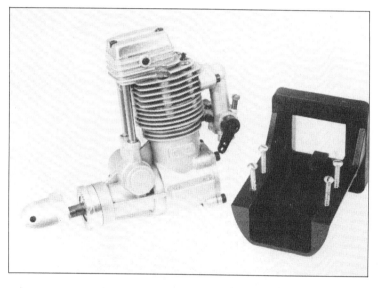

engines. A 4-ounce tank could be just right for a sport .20 engine, but it's barely enough for a .25. Anything larger than a .25 will need at least a 6-ounce tank, and in the .40 2-stroke range, an 8-ounce tank wouldn't be too big. Then again, the same size 4-stroke engine could get by nicely on a 4-ounce tank!

Wheels

Changes in wheel size aren't as dramatic as

Top: Engines use different types of engine mounts. This 4-stroke engine needs a longer mount than a 2-stroke of the same displacement.

Left: With few exceptions, the modeler must supply a fuel tank to even the best kit. The selection in most hobby shops is good, and there's a tank to fit every airplane.

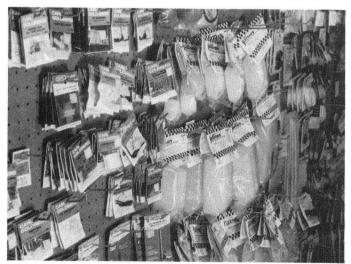

those in engine mounts and fuel tanks, but they should be taken into consideration. If an airplane with a .20-size engine is to be flown off a paved surface, it can use somewhat smaller wheels than one being flown off a grass field. The same airplane with a larger engine will require more ground clearance for its larger propeller. A difference of $1/2$ inch in the diameter of a wheel can make a big difference to a plane's ability to land and take off from various surfaces.

The three items I've mentioned require varied support hardware. The engine must be attached to the mount, and the mount to the firewall—usually with bolts and blind-nuts. The larger the engine, the larger the bolts and nuts.

The fuel tank must be connected to the engine and filler system with metal tubing and a flexible fuel line. Their size depends on the size and demands of the engine. (There are two sizes to consider in the .20 to .45 range.)

The wheels are usually held on the axles by wheel collars, but, since we're talking about only one landing gear, only one size of collar is necessary!

Can you see why manufacturers leave some choices to you? Unfortunately, acquiring the hardware necessary to complete a kit can be an almost insurmountable challenge for a beginner. Consider the problem of buying pushrods, clevises, control horns, hinges, linkages, etc., for kits that include a list rather than the parts! Ask your local hobby shop owner for advice when you're buying your first kit. We all have to start somewhere! ■

Wheels—some kits provide them, but most don't. Consider field conditions when making your selection.

C ontrol surfaces can be connected to a servo in a number of ways. The most positive way to transfer servo motion is through cables that make a "closed loop," starting from one servo-arm hole to a control horn on one side of the control surface, then from a horn on the other side of the control surface back to the opposite side of the servo arm. The cable system works well, but it has some drawbacks and is difficult to install and adjust. For this reason, pushrod systems are more popular. Let's look at the screw, or, more precisely, threads and their associated devices.

A pushrod with a threaded stud at one end that accepts a matching clevis is the most convenient way of transferring servo movement to a control surface. The threads allow the clevis to be screwed in or out to achieve very fine surface adjustments.

Threads and clevises aren't all alike, even though they're machined for 2-56 threads!

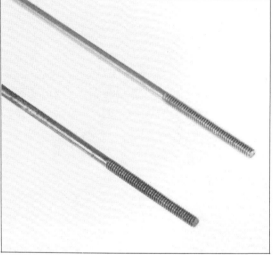

Which two of these clevises are the best? Bet you missed it! (See text.)

There are a several ways to produce threads on metal, but the two most usually found on pushrod ends are cut threads and rolled threads.

● Cut threads are made just as the term implies. The threads are cut into metal (usually steel) with a device called a "die," which has been made for wire of a specific size and with a specific number of threads per inch. Metal is removed to make a groove that spirals along the wire. The material between these grooves forms the threads. This is the most common way to generate threads.

● Rolled threads are made by a tool that presses the grooves into the metal and allows the material to rise on each side and form threads. No material is removed when threads are made in this way, and rolled threads are mandatory for all threaded fittings on full-scale aircraft.

The photograph shows the difference between rolled threads and cut threads. You'll see that the rolled threads on the end of the wire on the left have a larger diameter than the wire, while the cut threads on the other wire are of the same diameter as the wire. It's recommended that pushrod ends have rolled threads if at all possible, and this is especially true of larger and high-performance airplanes.

Any discussion of threaded pushrods would be incomplete without mention of the clevises (the reason for the threads' existence). The clevis can be the weakest link in the pushrod control system. The picture shows three types of clevis; all are more than strong enough for their intended purpose. Of the three, the nylon one is most likely to fail first, because of the pin shearing, but this would only happen under loads that far exceed the loads it's likely encounter in R/C applications!

The most important part of the clevis system isn't the clevis at all; it's the threaded rod that screws into the shank of the clevis. If there's any slop in the coupling (as is frequently the case with some of the imported threaded rods), don't use it! If the connection isn't tight, you're just inviting the clevis to part company with the rod when extreme loads are placed upon it. At best, this would change the trim, and at worse, the pushrod could pull completely out of the clevis and cause a loss of control.

Sudden, unusual increases in load don't always happen when the plane is airborne, but more often occur during everyday handling and trips to and from the field. Any time a control surface is moved by some external force, the load placed on the clevis-pushrod system can be much greater than anything experienced during flying.

Give all pushrod-clevis joints a dose of thin CA after trim has been established. (This is especially necessary if you use a straight-seam metal clevis.) You should also slip safety locks made of fuel tubing over all clevises that aren't self-locking.

Pushrod ends and clevises are very inexpensive, so use only the best. I also recommend that clevises and control horns be changed every year and that you never use any hardware that has been salvaged from a crash. It may have been its cause! ■

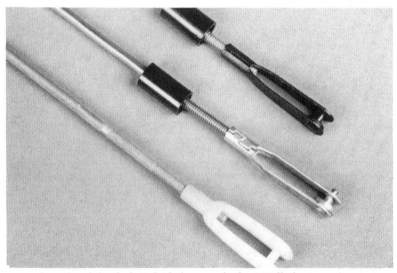

These threaded rods don't look the same do they? Well, they're not!

They're basic to wings

Ribs are the basic components of wings. They determine the airfoil, the thickness and width of the wing and the locations of the leading edge, the spars and the trailing edge, which are the load-carrying members. Even when making foam wings, we use airfoil templates that look like ribs to produce the desired shape and size.

Most modern kits include pre-formed ribs for your convenience, but if you prefer to build from plans, you'll find that forming ribs isn't as difficult as it seems. I'll describe two methods: one for those with access to power equipment, and the other for those of us who use only a modeling knife and a straightedge.

Making Ribs

First, make an accurate rib template. Trace the outline of the rib onto thin paper, glue it to heavy cardboard stock and then cut out the template. The plastic that's packed with sliced bacon is excellent for making templates; because it's semi-transparent, the rib outline can be traced through it, and the finished template is quite durable. Remember to check the accuracy of your template after you've made it.

If you have a belt (or disc) sander and a band saw, multiple rib blanks can be cut from balsa, stacked, pinned together and finished all at the same time. Just pin the template to the top of the stack and sand to the outline. Then, using a band saw, cut the spar notches and the leading and trailing edges into the shaped block. Remove the pins to reveal the completed ribs!

Using the template to make a printed sheet of ribs (by tracing around it on sheet balsa with a fine-tip pen) has two advantages over

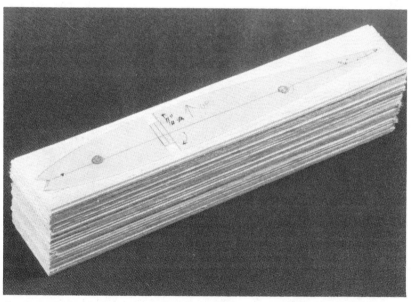

Stacking rib blanks, then sanding and sawing them to outline is one way to make ribs— but not the only way!

the sand-and-saw method: no power equipment is necessary, and one sheet of balsa will produce more ribs, thereby reducing your building costs. The only disadvantage is that it takes a little longer.

When tracing the rib outlines, careful placement of the template will conserve balsa and make cutting faster and easier. Ribs with flat bottoms can be drawn on the straight edges of the sheet or separated by a line. If the spar notches are matched, they can be cut into two ribs at once. Alternate the ribs' wide parts with the more slender trailing edges to make use of wood that would usually be trimmed away. This rib placement is like a jigsaw puzzle and can be treated as a game with only one rule: in every rib, the grain should run lengthwise!

Trim the ribs from the sheet with a sharp, pointed, razor knife and follow these simple rules:
● Cut on the line, or as close to it as you can.
● Hold the knife perpendicular to the balsa sheet and use a metal straightedge for the straight lines.
● Cut so that if the grain of the wood split or guided the blade, it would be away from the part. For example: to cut the top camber of the rib, slice from the top spar notch toward the

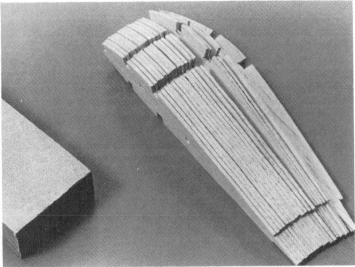

Left: It's difficult to tell sliced ribs that have been pinned together and sanded from those made with power equipment!

trailing edge, then from the notch toward the leading edge.

● It's easier to cut all the spar notches first, then the leading and trailing edges, and finally the outlines.

When all the ribs have been cut out, pin them together, put scrap spar material into the notches and sand them all to the same shape with a sanding block. This will smooth any uneven places and result in accurate ribs.

If you plan to cover the finished model with plastic film, why not drill some holes in the ribs while they're pinned together? This will let the film "breathe" through the tips (or servo well), and it will prevent it from ballooning when it's heat-shrunk.

This is a great sport, and all aspects of it should be fun! ■

A metal straightedge and a sharp knife are great for slicing ribs from a printed sheet.

Tracing rib outlines on sheet balsa and cutting them out takes time, but it saves a lot of material.

You could learn to fly R/C without an instructor, especially if you know how the controls operate and affect your airplane's flight path and if you have a solid, stable trainer like the Twiliter (see the March '87 *Model Airplane News*). It's much better, however, to enlist the aid of a good instructor.

Most of us old-timers learned to fly R/C by the crash-and-burn method. Fortunately, airplanes then were free-flight machines that took care of themselves. When a new flier appeared at the field, we never thought of offering help—that would have been an insult. It was assumed that he could learn just like the rest of us! I'm glad that times have changed.

Radios have changed, too, and so has the performance of engines and airplanes. Today's radio equipment can give your scale airplane much the same characteristics as the most advanced fighter! Even so-called "trainers" have a performance level that far exceeds the best combat airplanes of WW II. Who would climb into the cockpit of a full-scale airplane like that without lots of instruction and preliminary flight time?!

It's obvious that flight training should begin before you invest in a radio, an airplane, or an engine, but innocent "victims" still appear at flying fields with a shiny Super-Slipper 90 and a brand-new radio (on the only unusable frequency at the field) looking for help with their first flight! Naturally, someone comes to their rescue, but is that person the right someone?

Ask questions. Your dealer should know if there's a club in your area that offers instruction. Look for information in every local hobby shop, craft, discount, or hardware store that sells modeling supplies.

When you find a club, join, and talk to the officers; they're usually the ones with the most experience, and they can probably recommend a good instructor. When you have a good instructor, follow his advice when buying your equipment.

Training School

The R/C flight schools provide training airplanes, qualified instructors and a complete ground school. They aren't expensive when compared to the cost of an airplane, a radio and support equipment, but it usually takes at least a week to complete the course, and the cost doesn't include room and board. I know

Here are some of the many teaching videotapes available on the subject of aeromodeling.

of only one such school—the 1st U.S. R/C Flight School, 521 S. Sawyer, Shawano, WI 54166.

If you don't have a local flight school, join a club and ask members for advice! They'll be happy to help.

Training Videos

The latest training aids can be used as you sit in the comfort of your favorite armchair—training videotapes. The photo shows four of those available.

From the Milt Video Library comes "How To Build and Fly a Radio Controlled Model Airplane"—in this case, the PT-40 from Great Planes. It's a complete instructional tape that shows you how to build and fly that first plane.

InVenture Inc's. "Flight Training Program" tells you to "Get on the sticks...and fly right!" Recognizing that crashes discourage beginners, this video concentrates on flight training, field procedures and safety.

"How to Build and Fly Radio-Control Models" is by Mike Mas, who was the AMA National Helicopter Champion for four consecutive years. This tape helps you to select equipment and build a model, and it takes you through learning to fly and even perform maneuvers—loops, rolls, etc.

Finally, for the day when you're ready to try helicopters, "Model Helicopter Building and Flying Techniques" from Milt Video Library shows you how. Look for the addresses of these companies at the end of this book.

In aeromodeling, you need never be without help. ■

A very vital angle

The term "dihedral" comes from solid geometry, and it refers to the angle at which two planes join. In aircraft, the dihedral angle is that formed between the wing panel and the horizontal.

Two degrees of dihedral in a wing means that the wing tip is raised until it's at a 2-degree angle with the horizontal reference line. The dihedral angle can be either positive or negative, but the term "dihedral" usually indicates a positive number, and "anhedral" or "cathedral" indicates a negative one.

Dihedral is employed to increase an aircraft's stability. Assume an airplane is flying in a straight line at a fixed speed and constant altitude and that its flight path is upset by a gust of wind under its left wing. The left wing will rise and the airplane will slip toward the right, but, because of the dihedral, the slip causes the right wing to be at a higher angle of attack than the left, thereby generating more lift, which raises the right wing and returns the airplane to level flight. Other factors are involved, but this is the classic description of the effect of dihedral in stabilizing an airplane.

The effect of a "slip" on an airplane with dihedral is to make an R/C airplane bank without using ailerons. Two-channel (rudder and elevator) R/C airplanes rely on the rudder and dihedral to turn; rudder alone won't give the desired result. The action of the rudder and dihedral to cause a "bank" (necessary for a turn) can be seen in the following example of a left turn.

When the left-rudder command is given for a left turn, the rudder moves the tail to the right, so causing the airplane to slip forward toward its right side and bringing the right wing to a higher angle of attack (thus generating more lift for that wing). Unlike the momentary gust of wind in the previous example, the left rudder is held, and this keeps the airplane slipping and the right wing rising until the

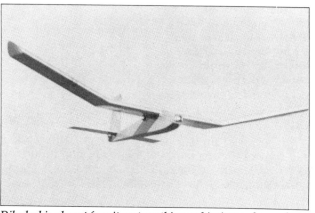

Dihedral is almost free: it costs nothing and isn't very heavy, but a rudder airplane won't turn without it.

desired banking angle is achieved. If the rudder is held longer, the airplane will eventually roll. As a general rule, 5 degrees of dihedral is considered adequate for rudder-elevator airplanes.

The effect of dihedral can be achieved in a variety of ways. An airplane with its wing above the thrust line will act as though it has 2 degrees more dihedral than it actually has. Conversely, an airplane with its wing below the thrust line can lose 2 degrees of effective dihedral. This accounts for the large increase of measured dihedral in low-wing airplanes that must rely on rudder-dihedral effect for control.

Sweep-back in a wing also causes an effect like that of dihedral, but for a slightly different reason. In a slip, the advancing swept-back wing presents its leading edge squarely to the airstream and achieves higher lift than the receding wing. A wing with a tapered (spanwise) leading edge will exhibit this characteristic to a lesser degree, and there's even some slight effect in a double tapered wing.

In theory, elliptical dihedral is the most efficient because there are no angular breaks in the lifting surfaces. At one time, an R/C sailplane with beautiful elliptical dihedral built into its wings was marketed, but construction difficulties have limited the use of this type of dihedral.

Next in line are wings with polyhedral and tip dihedral; these attempt to improve the efficiency of the lifting surface by approaching the elliptical. Most highly efficient sailplanes employ polyhedral wings, but most R/C aircraft use simple dihedral with the angle change at the fuselage where it can be adequately braced.

It's interesting that flat, very low-aspect-ratio wings show a stabilizing effect that resembles several degrees of dihedral. Shades of the flying saucer! ■

What does what

So far, I've discussed how to make the controls of an aircraft move; now it's time to see what happens when they move!

An airplane operates in three dimensions: up, down and sideways. (Time, or speed, isn't usually mentioned here.).Textbooks describe aircraft controls as those affecting:

- pitch (elevator)
- roll (aileron)
- yaw (rudder)
- power (throttle).

Let's see what these controls do. For this discussion, assume that the transmitter is two-stick configured for Mode II operation so the elevator and aileron are controlled by the right-hand stick, and the rudder and throttle are controlled by the one on the left. (All airplane controls interact.)

Elevator

The elevator controls the speed of the airplane. When the elevator-control stick on the transmitter is moved aft (toward the flier), the elevator on the airplane goes up, and so does the airplane's nose. This increases the wing's angle of attack, and causes more drag (and lift), so the airplane slows down.

Throttle

The throttle controls the airplane's altitude. In the previous description, if no other changes are made, the airplane will zoom up to a slightly higher altitude as its speed decreases; then it will settle into a nose-high flight attitude at a lower speed. If the throttle is advanced, the airplane will continue to climb at the same speed as before. The additional power overcomes the drag caused by the higher angle of attack (higher lift) assumed by the wing.

Conversely, when the power is reduced (throttle stick aft), the elevator control must be pushed forward (down-elevator) to maintain speed, and the airplane descends. Landings are made by reducing power, allowing the airplane to descend, then adding aft stick (up-elevator) to reduce speed as the airplane nears the ground.

Rudder

When rudder control alone is given, the airplane tries to skew or skid around, instead of banking smoothly. The rudder works in the same way as the elevator, but horizontally: the rudder goes left, the nose goes left, etc. When the rudder moves, the flight path tends to remain a straight line, even though the nose is now pointed in a different direction. It will continue to slip sideways, unless there's enough dihedral in the wings to cause the more forward wing to generate more lift and initiate a bank.

Aileron

The aileron doesn't work in the same way as the elevator and rudder: when one goes up, the other goes down. The down-aileron causes a change in the wing's airfoil and generates

The controls can't control the airplane unless the transmitter controls the controls! Always check control response before any flight.

more lift on that side. The up-aileron causes more drag on the other wing, and this results in loss of lift, so the airplane banks toward the up-aileron wing.

When aileron control alone is given, before the airplane starts to bank towards the up-aileron, it yaws toward the down-aileron, because the down-aileron causes more drag than the one that goes up! This effect is called "adverse yaw." Proper aileron design and servo set-up go a long way toward reducing this effect, and only very large models require coordinated rudder and aileron control (i.e., simultaneous left aileron and left rudder).

Turning

Whether the airplane uses three or four channels for control, there's no difference in the turning procedure. In 3-channel airplanes, the rudder works with the wing dihedral to produce a turn in much the same way as the ailerons in a 4-channel bird.

Remember, I said that all controls interact, so in a turn, there's more than one directional movement of the stick.

First, establish a bank angle. For a left turn, the left wing is slanted downward while the right wing goes up. Because there's now less lift supporting the airplane, you must increase the wing's angle of attack to overcome this loss of lift. Once these parameters have been established, the airplane will remain in a banked turn, at the same altitude, until it's affected by an outside force, or given another control.

To recover from a turn, the wings must be brought back to level, and, because the lift is now directed upward instead of at an angle, the additional lift is no longer required, so the angle of attack must be reduced. How do we alter this angle of attack? Easy!

In practice, a left turn is performed by moving the stick on the right side of the transmitter to the left until a bank has been achieved. Then, since no more bank angle is necessary, the stick is moved backward slightly to add some up-ele-

Right: The elevator controls the airplane's speed. The up-elevator on this 1/4-scaler raises the wing to a high angle of attack, slowing the airplane just before touchdown. This is the way all landings should be made.

Left: Airplanes that rely on rudder for directional control require more dihedral to cause a bank because of the yawing motion induced by the rudder. With proper design, 3-channel airplanes can be made to turn almost as smoothly as those equipped with ailerons.

Above: A properly banked turn. Notice the ailerons in neutral and the slight amount of up-elevator that holds altitude. The steeper the bank, the more elevator and power are necessary to overcome the G-forces exerted on the airplane.

vator and maintain altitude. To recover from the turn, move the stick to the right, level the wings, and release the back stick so that the airplane can regain level flight.

Let's look at the top of the stick while we execute a left turn. It moves in an arc from center straight left, then around and back, on around to the right, then forward and, finally, straight back to center. A right turn is executed in the same way, but it's started by moving the stick right, then back and around to left, finally arriving at neutral center.

When flying, this becomes one smooth movement, and you hardly realize that you're moving the stick, because you're thinking about the airplane, not the stick. Airplanes are stupid and stubborn, and they must be forced to do what you want them to do; but they prefer to fly, rather than crash (a condition that's inevitably pilot-induced! See Chapter 33).

It won't fly if it isn't balanced

To fly correctly, an airplane must be in proper trim. In this case, "trim" refers to a condition of the flying surfaces (the wing, vertical fin and horizontal stabilizer) and to the position of the control surfaces (the ailerons, rudder and elevator) that allow the airplane to maintain a straight and level flight path without continuous control input. A properly trimmed airplane is a pleasure to fly.

Balance

The first consideration is balance. The plans or instructions that come with an airplane kit or construction article usually show a range in which the balance point or center of gravity (CG) should be found. In the absence of instructions, and assuming a conventional-type airplane configuration, a point at 25 percent of the wing chord aft of the leading edge (measured at the wing root) is a good place to start. Weight must occasionally be added to the nose or tail to bring the plane into a slightly nose-down pitch attitude.

Proper balance depends on more than just fore-and-aft adjustment. The density of the construction materials and the mounting systems of the engine and radio and their locations, can cause wide variations in lateral (side-to-side) balance as well. It's therefore important to balance the airplane along its fuselage center line by adding weight to the tip of its lighter wing. If you add weight internally, before covering the airplane, you'll avoid having to dig into the wing after completing the plane.

Warps

Before flying it, you must inspect your airplane and correct any warps in its flying surfaces. If a heat-shrink plastic was used for covering, you'll usually be able to eliminate warps with a heat gun or a hair dryer. Just hold the surface straight while heating it, or pull slightly against the warp.

When all the warps have been removed, center the rudder, and rig the elevator and ailerons flush with the bottom of the surface to which they're joined.

The Test Flight

On the first test flight, you should achieve rough-level flight trim and see whether surface throws are adequate to maintain positive control of direction and elevation. On subsequent flights, the control surfaces should be reset at the servo or clevis ends so that the transmitter trim levers can be returned to center and final trimming can begin.

First, put the airplane into level flight, and

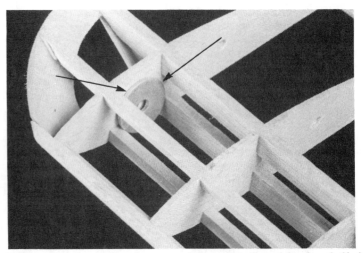

Differences in the wood used can cause differences in the weight of one half of a wing. A metal washer glued to the tip rib of this wing solved the problem.

adjust the elevator and aileron trim levers on the transmitter until the plane's flight remains constant "hands off." Now, do two or three consecutive loops directly in front of you and into the wind. If the airplane moves away from you, the wing closest to you is lighter than the other; if the airplane moves toward you, the wing nearest you is the heavy one. Land; add weight to the light wing; trim for level flight; and try the loops once more. Repeat this procedure until the airplane tracks straight through at least three loops.

Once lateral balance has been achieved, return the airplane to level flight and reduce the throttle to the lowest setting that will maintain altitude. Trim the elevator and rudder for level flight, then advance the throttle and re-trim—this time, with the aileron and the elevator.

This trimming procedure assumes that the airplane's thrust line is correct. An offset thrust line can amplify trim problems and, in some cases, make proper trim impossible. Thrust changes are invaluable with free-flying airplanes, but they should only be used as a last resort for R/C aircraft.

All the airplane's controls interact, and if the preceding steps are repeated once more, a compromise should be reached and your typical sport (or training) airplane should be properly trimmed. There! You're ready to go! ■

To fly correctly, an airplane must be properly balanced. Made of a wooden block and two 1/2-inch dowels, this simple fixture is ideal.

Why we need to know about it

Balance: state of equipoise, as between weights, different elements, or opposing forces; equilibrium; steadiness." This definition from Mr. Webster is almost ideal as far as the balance of a model airplane is concerned.

The term "center of gravity," or CG, refers to the point at which all the weight of an airplane is completely balanced. The actual point is a little difficult to locate, but the extension of a line through that point on the airplane's horizontal and lateral axes is of great importance. On our plans, that little circle with "CG" written on it tells us where we should balance our airplane when the wings and fuselage are level.

Each airfoiled wing has a certain angle of attack at which it has the most lift with the least amount of drag. To make this work in

This airplane will be fun to fly and easy to control because it has been properly balanced.

our favor, the wing is mounted on the fuselage at an angle that will allow it to operate at its best while the fuselage offers the least amount of drag and the wing is at this optimum angle.

The horizontal tail is set at the proper angle of attack to allow the wing to maintain this angle while in flight. The aircraft is balanced so that these parameters can be maintained while it's in stable, level flight. This situation produces the most efficient use of power to overcome drag while flying.

In the last paragraph, one word is of major importance—"stable." Stability allows an airplane to fly for long periods. A very unstable airplane will fly, but its airborne time will usually be very short and its landing catastrophic! Stability is achieved by the proper size and design of the flight surfaces, the wing and the tail, and the correct location of the center of balance.

An airplane that's nose-heavy is more stable than a tail-heavy one. A nose-heavy airplane becomes increasingly stable as more and more weight is added to the nose, until it's so stable

that it's uncontrollable and won't fly. Conversely, an airplane becomes more and more unstable as it becomes more and more tail-heavy, until it, too, reaches a point where it's uncontrollable and won't fly. The result is the same whether an airplane is balanced too far forward or too far aft, but control is lost much sooner as the balance point is shifted toward the tail.

Some types of free-flying, indoor, rubber-powered models are balanced as far aft as the trailing edge of the wing and, in some cases, even further back! This is done because the airplane is expected to fly in a controlled airspace with very limited changes in attitude. They're "set" in the air by their pilots, and they climb at a gentle rate in a fixed circle. If their flight path is upset beyond a certain limit, they become unstable and flight ends. This situation is fine for a very light indoor model that suffers no damage from occasional crashes, but it's out of the question for R/C airplanes!

For most of the model airfoils in conventional aircraft, the proper balance point is a point that's between 25 and 30 percent of the distance aft of the leading edge of the average cord. This is usually, but not always, the location of the main spar and the thickest part of the wing. With the balance established within this range, the airplane is stable and easy to control.

An airplane with very rapid response to small elevator and rudder control movements is tail-heavy and almost impossible to land. An airplane that can't be stalled with full elevator control is nose-heavy and also difficult to land. An airplane in proper balance is beautiful, graceful and a pleasure to fly because of the smooth response to control inputs.

Any new model should be balanced as called for in the plans. Since no two airplanes ever come out the same, after the test flights, try making slight alterations to the balance to arrive at the just right point for this particular airplane. If it seems to be nose-heavy, add small amounts of clay to the tail, and weighted prop washers, made for the purpose, can be added to the nose. Somewhere, there's a point that's just right for every model.

There's one more balancing job: your plane must balance laterally. Balance it down the center line of the fuselage by adding weight to the lighter wing tip, or making the heavier one lighter. ∎

There are almost as many types of landing gear and ways to install them as there are kinds of airplanes. Retracts, which are popular for scale and pattern aircraft, have never become commonplace among sport fliers. In sport flying, fixed gears predominate, and the most popular are made from sheet aluminum and steel wire, each of which has its particular advantages.

Above: Wing-mounted, torsion-bar landing gear. The torsion bar can be recessed into the wing for a smoother installation.

Right: The same gear showing the mount from the inside! Mounts like these are simple, but take a lot of punishment.

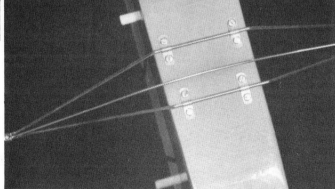

springy. The nose gear of a tricycle-geared airplane is invariably made of steel wire with a two- or three-turn spring near the mounting to provide for a "knee" type of action. These nose gear are almost indestructible and rarely require adjustment.

Music-wire main gear fall into two general categories: torsion and bolt-on types.

● **The torsion gear** is so named because, under impact, its design places a twisting load on the wire. Because the load is applied to a relatively long piece, it's easily absorbed, and the wire will return to its original position.

Mountings for this type of gear are slightly more com-

plicated than for simple bolt-on gear, but they can be smaller and lighter because the gear itself (rather than the mount) absorbs the load on landing. The gear legs are easy to make: each requires only three bends of 90 degrees or less. Torsion gear can be mounted on the fuselage or in the wings, depending on what your aircraft's design calls for.

● **Bolt-on wire gear** are almost always mounted on the fuselage because they require a fore-and-aft separation of the mounting points. Even though a gear is formed from a single piece of wire, it must be bent to provide this mounting separation.

Twin strut gear lend themselves to this type

Formed-Aluminum Gear

Formed-aluminum gear are the easiest to install because they're simply bolted to the bottom of the fuselage. Although they're made of tempered-aluminum stock, which is quite hard, they usually have to be straightened after a few hard landings. This isn't a real problem and can be easily avoided by using steel-wire cross-bracing.

Steel-Wire Gear

Gear made of steel wire are by far the most popular fixed gear. They're inexpensive, easy to install and quite durable because the wire is of mount. Both struts can be of smaller wire than would be necessary for a single leg, and the spacing offers the ideal fore-and-aft separation for mounting. Fairings between the struts not only offer a scale-like appearance, but also reduce the drag of the open wire.

Formed-aluminum gear take bolt-on wheels, some of which have threaded bosses into which the axles, with wheels, are bolted. Others have holes drilled for axles that are then bolted into place with a screw and nut. Wheels should never ride on the threads of the mounting screws, but on smooth axles held in place by the screws. To ensure this, slide a section of brass or aluminum tubing over the bolt axles to make a smooth surface on which the wheel hub will ride.

Wheel Installation

Music-wire gear offer two methods of wheel installation: collars or soldered washers.

• **Wheel collars,** which are available in all popular sizes, offer the easiest installation because they require no additional tools. Place a collar on both sides of the wheel to keep it centered on the axle.

• **Brass washers** that fit the wire offer excellent wheel mounting when soldered into place, but if you aren't familiar with soldering techniques, use the wheel-collar method.

Just remember that well-designed, well-installed gear make good landings look great and allow you to taxi away from the bad ones! ■

Left: The bolt-on wire gear is more complicated than torsion gear, but smaller wire can be used, and the mount is simply a plywood plate in the fuselage bottom.

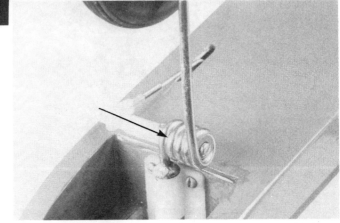

Almost without exception, nose gear are made with a two- or three-turn spring to give a "knee" action that absorbs the shock of nose-first landings!

Some necessities and some luxuries

You must do some planning before you take your new trainer on that first trip to the field. If, like most modelers, you fly at a site that's far from your workshop, you should take along certain items to the field…just in case. First, you need something in which to carry everything, and this can be as simple as a cardboard box! That's your "flight box." Let's see what equipment you'll need.

Only three things are absolutely necessary for engine-powered airplanes: fuel, a starting battery and a transmitter, but let's look more closely at these basic necessities.

Fuel

Fuel in a can is of little use unless you have some way to pump, pour or squirt it into your plane's tank! You could use a small funnel or an eye dropper, but they aren't practical. A pump and some tubing to connect it to the tank make a much better arrangement. Both hand-operated and electric pumps work well, so check magazine advertisements to find out what's available.

A Starting Battery

Next on the list is the starting battery. (Having a dead battery is very frustrating, so most experienced fliers carry a spare.) A 1.5V dry cell with the proper glow-plug connector will work, but not for long. A glow-plug is a high-current device, but dry cells are made for low-current use. A Ni-Cd starting battery with a connector and a charger isn't expensive, and it will outlast thousands of dry cells!

A Transmitter

A transmitter is the last of the basic three. This seems so obvious that it should go without saying, but everyone who flies has left his transmitter at home at least once. Your trans-mitter should have a proper frequency flag, so that others fliers can note what frequency you're using. Remember, never turn on your transmitter until you're sure your frequency is clear. Every field has some sort of frequency control, so find out what it is and use it!

More Handy Gadgetry

Those are the essentials, but there are other things that will help you spend more time in the air. Propellers and glow plugs are expendable, so spares in the proper sizes should be included in your flight box. The person who goes to the field with only one prop is almost sure to break it, but when there's a spare in his box, it will last for weeks! The same is true of glow plugs. When the engine fails to start, first check the battery. If it makes a new plug light up, it's OK. Next, check the engine plug; if it doesn't glow, replace it, and don't forget to replace the spare on your next trip to the hobby shop!

Your flight box should contain all the support equipment you'll need for a day at the field. This one has a drawer for small parts and partitions for fuel, starter, transmitter, etc.

You need wrenches to install and remove propellers and glow plugs. By far the handiest is a four-way wrench that can handle a variety of prop nuts and glow plugs. On some engines, the plug is recessed deeply into the head, and a rather thin-walled socket is necessary for its replacement. Check your engine to find the correct size of prop and plug wrenches.

Before every flying session, check all engine screws and nuts and tighten them, if necessary. Carry screwdrivers and Allen wrenches that match the nuts on your engine and mount. A pair of pliers, extra rubber bands, fuel line and a knife will also come in handy.

Splurge a Little!

We've covered the necessities; now let's talk luxuries! An electric starter with a 12V motorcycle battery (or Ni-Cd pack) comes to mind. A "chicken stick" is the next best thing, and it's a big help for cranking in winter when engines tend to be hungry for fingers!

A big, soft towel and a spray bottle filled with window cleaner make after-flying clean-up much easier. A starting battery with a meter to read plug current is useful; even better would be a 12V system that can provide, and meter, all power requirements and can recharge transmitter and receiver batteries as well!

Then there are wind-speed and -direction indicators, drink coolers, portable barbecues, a tent, motor generator.... A flight box can get out of hand! ∎

Left: This box might be called a "flight-line box" because it holds only a starter, props and fuel. Boxes like this are typical of those used by contest fliers; they complement the regular flight box.

Below: Associated with spare glow plugs, pliers and wrenches is a reamer, which is very handy if you forgot to drill out that new prop to fit your engine's crankshaft before leaving home.

Simple tests that make a difference

Test-flying a new airplane is always a thrill; sometimes, however, the desire to get to that phase is so strong that we overlook poorly fitting joints and sloppy assembly in our rush to get the airplane into the air.

Let's look at preflight testing in a slightly different way. Almost everything we do when we build and assemble an airplane is a test, and we perform hundreds of them during construction. Two of the most common tests are comparing the sizes of wooden pieces and fitting pieces before we glue them into place. Most of these tests are done without conscious thought; they're an automatic part of building an airplane. Just a few more tests won't take up much more time—and they might save a lot of that commodity later on!

When you lift the wing from the plan (but before you sand it), check it for warps. If you find any, get rid of them. Do this by spraying the balsa structure with alcohol, then pin the wing to a flat surface until it's dry.

Washout & Warps

One kind of warp is good: it's called "washout," and it's a condition where the the tip of the trailing edge is slightly higher than the leading edge, resulting in a lower angle of attack at the tip. A small amount of washout in the wing panels is fine—if it's the same in both panels. This type of warp results in a straight-ahead stall with less tendency to fall off on a wing.

Before covering any surface, sand everything that will come into contact with the covering material. This important step helps to prevent warping when the covering is tightly shrunk. After covering, check for warps once more, and remove them by heating the surface with a heat gun or iron while pulling gently against the warp. Result: warp-free

wings that will contribute to a smooth test flight.

After the fuselage has been framed-up, check to see that it's straight and that the wing

It's much better to start the preflight inspection at this stage of construction, rather than at the field just before the first flight! This is the Scrap Stick designed by John Gill.

saddle and stab mount are at right angles to the fuselage sides and parallel to each other. The easiest way to do this is by laying 3-foot lengths of $1/4$-inch balsa across the wing saddle and the stab mount and comparing them to the fuselage sides and to each other. If they square and parallel, this is the best time to make corrections.

Mount the engine on the firewall and check that the line of thrust is the same as that shown on the plans. Again, this is the best time to make corrections. For small corrections, metal washers under the engine mounting lugs or between the firewall and the engine mount are acceptable, but a flat, true firewall is best!

When gluing the stab and the rudder to the fuselage, make sure they're at right angles to each other and that the stab is firmly in its mount. (We know the mount is right because we've already checked it!) Only wood-to-wood joints are acceptable, so peel away any covering material in the areas that will be glued.

When the airplane has been completely covered (and while the fuel tank is empty), install the engine, landing gear and wheels. Use the servos, receiver and battery to achieve the balance point shown on the plans. Usually, if you place the battery as far forward as possible, you can correct tail-heavy situations. If it still won't balance, as a last resort, add weight to the nose or tail until it does.

When all the radio components have been installed, check for proper control response. Move the right stick backward and forward; the elevator should move up and down. Moving that stick to the right should make the right aileron go up and the left aileron go down; moving it to the left should make the left aileron go up and the right aileron go down. (On a 3-channel airplane, the left and right movement should cause the rudder to move left and right instead.)

The left stick controls the throttle; push it forward for high engine and pull it back for idle. For a 4-channel airplane, left and right rudder is actuated by this stick when it's moved left and right. Change sides of the servo-output arms with the pushrods until all these movements have been achieved. Or, if your radio is relatively new and has a servo-reversing feature on its transmitter, move the switches to the positions that give the commanded direction of throw.

Fill the tank with fuel and run the engine several times to establish the proper starting sequence. Hold the airplane at different attitudes and check that it runs properly. Before going to the field, check the control responses with the engine at all throttle settings.

At the field, a range check is the only remaining preflight test; all the rest have been taken care of during construction. The first flight of a properly built and assembled airplane is the very best part of R/C modeling! ■

A no-surprises test flight is a very satisfying conclusion to any construction project. The Scrap Stick's construction was written up as a "serial" in the Dallas R/C Club's newsletter.

Vibration is a problem for anything powered by an internal-combustion engine. Other than crashes, it's the principal cause of the failure of model structures and equipment. If radios and battery packs aren't protected by layers of foam or other vibration-absorbent material, they don't function.

Vibration-Reducing Engine Mounts

Until now, model engine-mounting systems that dampened vibration were adapted from products designed for other applications. Mountings were costly and installation required ingenuity. Only those who fly the rough-running giants, and better pattern fliers who practice several hours a day, use them now.

A vibration-reducing engine mount greatly prolongs engine and equipment life. Look at the photo of the Snuf-Vibe from J'Tec. This vibration-reduction system is easy to install, inexpensive and effective. Two sizes are available: one for average sport engines and one for the larger engines that fit the bigger birds.

Using this product doesn't mean that vibration protection of vital radio parts can be neglected, but it will make these protection systems more effective. No radio system is 100-percent reliable, but every precaution should be taken, and it might make the difference between having an airplane or just an unpleasant memory at the end of a flying session!

Electric-powered airplanes don't suffer from vibration as much as gas-powered ships; some manufacturers of electric kits even recommend receiver- and battery-mounting systems that offer almost no protection. Although this type of mounting is usually sufficient, it doesn't hurt to add some foam around the receiver and flight battery.

The new dual-conversion narrow-band receiver, with its smaller receiving "window" and two crystals to determine its position in the radio spectrum, are even more vulnerable to vibration than the older wide-band types. Temperature changes can also cause changes in the operating frequency, or receiving window. Luckily, most vibration-dampening materials used around receivers also insulate from heat and cold! (Transmitters can suffer the same fate and shouldn't be subjected to temperature extremes.)

Flutter

While on the subject of vibration, we should consider a close relative, flutter, which can be described as an airflow-induced oscillation of one or more flight surface. It occurs most often in ailerons and elevator.

While vibration gradually causes deterioration in aircraft structures, flutter can be explosive in effect! It can destroy a surface in a matter of seconds, and the loss of a control surface in flight is almost always catastrophic.

The principal cause of flutter is slop or play

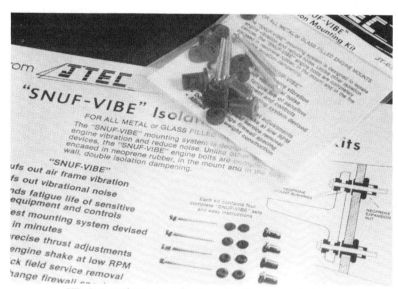

J'Tec's contribution to vibration reduction in our airplanes.

in the pushrod, control-horn, or servo-arm areas of the control surface. The holes in control horns must be a good solid fit for the clevis from the servo. Likewise, the pushrod clevis or connector should fit the servo arm securely. Hinge lines must be straight, with no binding

The home-built aircraft builders' bible is handy for modelers, too!

or play. If a surface distorts when it's actuated, this indicates a poor hinge line that should be corrected before you attempt a flight.

Flutter is a function of air speed, and its sound is unmistakable. When it's detected in flight, power and speed must be reduced immediately to minimize damage. The problematic surface should be corrected before flying is resumed. It's best to do it right the first time; you may not have a second chance! ■

Going where you want to go

Rudder and Elevator Movements

This chapter is for those who haven't been able to find a good instructor and complete a satisfactory solo flight. It isn't a flying course, but it describes the stick inputs needed to control an aircraft's basic attitudes. I'll consider two controls: the elevator for attitude and the rudder for heading. I'll assume that both of these controls are on the same stick.

I'll consider rudder and elevator movements from the transmitter's right-hand control stick. The same movements have the same effect on the aircraft's flight if ailerons replace the rudder in this configuration.

The surfaces on the airplane must correspond to the movement of the stick in the following way:
● When the stick is moved to the left, the trailing edge of the rudder also moves to the left.

● When the stick is moved to the right, the trailing edge of the rudder moves to the right.
● If you push the stick forward (away from you), the trailing edge of the elevator should move down.
● If you pull the stick back (toward you), the trailing edge of the elevator should move up.

It follows that if the stick is moved to the back left corner, the rudder should move to the left and the elevator should move up. Because the stick can be moved in a complete circle, all combinations of rudder and elevator movement, as well as the amount of deflection, can be obtained.

In flight, the elevator controls the wing's angle of attack. When the stick is moved back, the airplane's nose goes up and the airplane climbs because the wing generates more lift at a higher angle of attack. There's a price to pay for this additional lift: it reduces airspeed.

When the stick is moved to the left, the combination of left rudder and wing dihedral causes the airplane to bank to the left. If the rudder is held, the airplane will continue to bank until it enters a left-hand spiral dive. The airplane dives because when the wing is slanted toward the ground, the lift it generates is no longer against gravity, but at some other angle to the ground. Therefore, during all turns, more lift is necessary to maintain level flight.

This Sig Seniorita is in a steep right-hand bank. The left-rudder deflection indicates that the pilot has already provided control input to re-establish a "wings-level" attitude.

You can generate this lift by moving the stick back to obtain up-elevator, which increases the wing's angle of attack. The aircraft slows just as it does when it's in a climb, so it can stall in the same way in a turn as it can in a climb.

A Smooth Left Turn

To perform a smooth left turn without losing altitude, make the following stick movements:
● Move the stick to the left, and when the bank angle has been established, allow it to return to center. At the same time, pull the stick back to increase lift and maintain altitude.
● At the completion of the turn, move the stick to the right until the wings are again level and, at the same time, move it back to the center, as the extra lift is no longer needed.

During a turn, the stick actually follows a semicircle, which goes from the center to the left, then back, and finally around to the right before returning to the center.

A right turn is performed in the same way,

but it starts to the right and ends from the left back to center. In general, full-range movement of the stick isn't necessary, because the proper bank angle and elevator movement are usually obtained with much less than full deflection of the stick.

To correct heading differences caused by air currents, straight flight requires only occasional control inputs and is simply done by moving the stick slightly to the left or to the right as the situation demands. Corrections made when the aircraft is flying directly toward you can be confusing—unless you remember to "move that stick to that low wing to control that thing."

I hope that this discussion has made it a little easier for you to understand the effect of stick movement on an airplane's flight. The airplane already knows how to fly; the trick is to make it fly where you want it to go! It's relatively easy to learn, and once learned, it's never forgotten. ∎

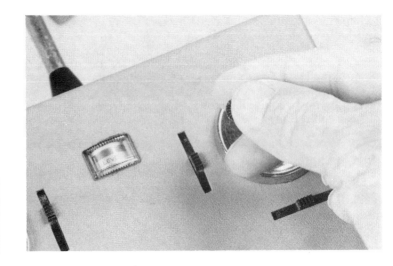

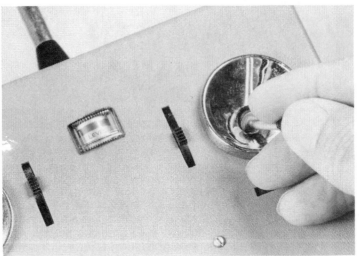

Above: These pictures show the sequence of stick movements needed to complete a left turn. First, move the stick to the left until the airplane assumes the proper bank angle...

Left: With bank angle established, move the stick back to provide the up-elevator necessary to prevent the airplane from diving in the turn...

Below: Finally, move the stick to the right to bring the wings level, and then move the stick back to center.

The First U.S. R/C Flight School has trained nearly 100 students, and the graduation rate is 96 percent! Every day for five days, each student receives about 6 hours of training, which includes more than 1 hour of flight time in 10- to 15-minute segments.

The school has two K&B .65 Sportster engines that have flown their trainers for more than 200 hours! One trainer has actually flown more than 13,000 miles without breaking down, and these impressive numbers prove the value of proper airplane maintenance.

Batteries

Even the smallest model represents a sizable investment in time and money, and, if properly maintained, it should deliver years of dependable performance. Before you go to the field, make sure that the radio batteries and engine-starting batteries are in good condition. Ni-Cd batteries lose the first 10 percent of their charge just a few hours after charging and at a slower rate thereafter. For charging depleted packs, allow at least 24 hours before a flying session, and allow at least a few hours for a booster charge on freshly charged packs.

Storage

If your model hangs from a ceiling or on a wall when not in use, dust it before a flying session! Dust on a model resembles frost on the wings of a full-scale aircraft: it causes drag and should be removed.

Wings

The free-flight practice of using rubber bands to hold wings on airplanes is still used because it helps to reduce crash damage. If the rubber bands aren't in good condition, replace them.

If nylon bolts are used for wing mounting, check them and check the condition of the threads in the blocks that receive them.

Control Systems

Inspect all pushrods, servo connectors and clevises. External control-horn-to-clevis connections are always suspect because they're exposed to exhaust residue, and they collect dust and grit from the propwash every time the engine is started or the airplane is taxied. The oily grit causes excess wear and enlarges the holes in the control horns. This causes slop in the control system, and this can lead to flutter, which is a very destructive condition. Checking control response before each flight should become automatic.

Check all engine, carburetor, muffler and prop-mounting bolts and the condition of the

Before leaving the field, run the engine and remove the fuel line so that all the fuel in the engine is used up.

fuel lines and tank. Finally, check your wheels for freedom of movement and tracking.

Most experienced R/Cers do these preflight chores automatically, because they know it's easier to fix a problem in the shop rather than at the field. When you've finished flying for the day, before you leave the field, start the engine, and while it's running, remove the fuel line so that the engine can burn all the fuel that's left in the crankcase.

Cleaning

It's important to clean the airplane thoroughly after every flight. Spray a good glass cleaner onto the airplane's surfaces, and wipe it off with clean paper towels to remove exhaust residue. Repeat this until no oil or dirt remains and the surfaces are clean, and remember to give special attention to clevises and landing gear. This is also a good time to fix any dings or holes in the covering material.

A spray bottle of alcohol is handy for cleaning the engine and engine compartment. First, to keep dirt from accidentally washing into this area, plug the carburetor air intake with a piece of paper towel. After washing, wipe the engine and surrounding area with paper towels until everything is clean and dry.

Give the engine a good dose of after-run oil, because the nitromethane in the fuel leaves an acid residue. Use Marvel Mystery Oil or a good automatic transmission fluid. To get oil into the engine, fill the carb intake with oil and flip the prop. Repeat this until all the bearings have been well lubricated. With 4-stroke engines, the oil should be injected into the exhaust and the crankcase breather vent to reach all the bearings. Between flying sessions, to protect the engine from dust, wrap it with a paper towel or a cloth. None of these chores takes long to do, and each should be part of every flying schedule. ■

Left: Seal the tank to eliminate the possibility of fuel leaks or contamination by cleaning fluids when you clean the engine.

Below: A good after-run oil is essential to prolong engine life. Work the oil into all engine bearings by flipping the prop several times.

How to avoid crashing

Here are the 10 most common reasons for the "I ain't got it" cry. Compiled by John Gill and based on an excerpt from a Dallas R/C Club Newsletter, the reasons for failure appears in ascending order of frequency.

10. An oil-contaminated receiver switch causes about 3 percent of failures. The solution, of course, is to keep oil away from the switch. Internally mounted switches that are activated from the side of the airplane away from the exhaust stack are best. Externally mounted switches must be on the non-exhaust side and higher, rather than lower, on the fuselage.

9. A broken wire to the servo or antenna also causes about 3 percent of failures. Before every flying session, part of your preflight inspection should include a good look at all the wiring and connectors. That broken wire could turn out to be the reason the aileron servo fails to respond to the receiver! Check all the controls before takeoff.

8. A receiver battery failure causes 3 percent of failures. This problem is more difficult to discover in advance because the voltage reading can be correct one minute and zero the next. Vibration and heat are battery killers—protect them from both! Replacing battery packs at the end of the season is very inexpensive insurance.

7. A bad or poor connection in the receiver switch causes 4 percent of failures. This is related to no. 10, and it can be caused by prolonged vibration. Good switches with positive on and off action that are wired in a redundant fashion should remain safe for several seasons.

6. A broken wire in or near the battery pack is in the 4-percent range of failures, too. Moving the battery pack while a voltmeter is attached to it should help you see this problem at once. Some time during each flying session, check for a flicker in the battery voltage while the engine is running.

5. A worn or dirty servo motor is another 4-percent problem. The motor and the gear train create problems in this area. When the action of the control surfaces is slower, or control response in the air seems different, the servos should be checked immediately. Servos do all the work on board the airplane, so replace them when they're tired!

4. A worn or dirty servo pot causes nearly 5 percent of all failures. The potentiometer (pot) in a servo is like a radio's volume control, but it follows the output arm and tells the electronics when the arm is in the place it was told to go. Dirty or worn pots cause jerky, erratic servo movement; worse yet, they cause radio noise that can make all the servos wiggle. To

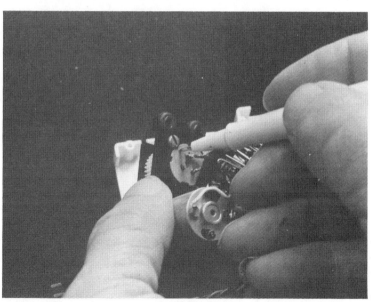

The pen points to the outside of the servo pot. A servo with a dirty pot can generate radio noise that causes the rest of the servos to "jitter."

find the faulty servo, connect them one at a time. When the culprit is found, have it serviced

3. Low transmitter voltage from a battery pack causes 16 percent of failures, and there's no excuse for this one. Most transmitters have voltmeters or output meters on the front. Expect 2 hours of flying time from a well-charged pack—that's 2 hours maximum with a well-charged pack.

2. Low receiver voltage from a battery pack destroys 25 percent of our planes! This is related to no. 3, but it isn't as easy to guard against because the receiver pack doesn't have a meter to tell us when things have gone too far. Servos require most of the current from the battery, so flights with a lot of control input drain the pack faster than those in which the airplane flies itself most of the time. For that reason, it's difficult to judge just how long a receiver pack will function. Don't try to make "just one more flight"!

The inside of the servo pot. Servos should be cleaned with a soft brush and a solvent—usually alcohol. Some require a light lubricant.

1. Pilot error is responsible for 30 percent of model airplane destruction. Here's what John Gill says:

"Obviously, pilot error is the number-one culprit in the destruction of our aircraft. Now, consider that to the 30-percent 'dumb thumb' statistic, we should add the numbers from 2 through 10 as easily precedented by the builder/pilot, the blame rate goes beyond 90 percent. That's 'cause for pause,' isn't it?

"Seriously, these numbers are pretty accurate. So if you'll try to carry out adequate maintenance and fly with reasonable caution, it's probable that you'll eliminate over 90 percent of your accidents. That translates to one possible crash in each 1,000 flights."

These are words to live by! ■

The cause of most model failures—the pilot!

Just in case you crash…!

Regular maintenance is an important part of keeping an airplane in flying condition. After every flying session, wipe the engine clean and squirt a good oil (e.g., Marvel Mystery) into the intake and exhaust ports. Check all mounting bolts and, if necessary, tighten them; inspect all the linkages; and

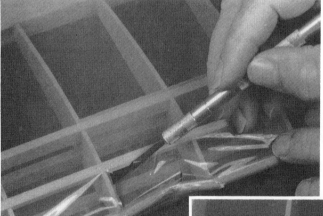

Above: When repairing a built-up, covered surface, first trim away the covering to expose the damaged structure.

Right: The damaged area must be replaced with new wood. Notice that, on each end, the old structure was trimmed away at an angle; this provides more area for gluing the replacement part.

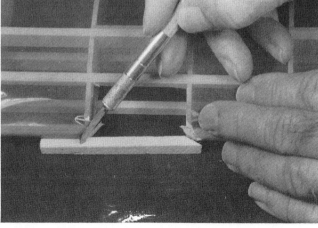

fences seem to jump in front of airplanes and leave their impressions in the leading edge! As long as the main spars are undamaged, repairs in this area aren't too difficult to make and, if made carefully, they're almost invisible.

●**Built-up wings.** These fall into two categories: those with leading-edge sheeting and those without, but these two types require almost the same technique to repair them. Sheeting provides extra strength, but its chief function is to keep the airfoil true between the ribs. For this reason, there are often two or more small spars just behind the leading edge.

First, cut the covering away from the top and bottom to expose the damage. Cut to the first undamaged ribs and back to the main spar, or wherever

clean the entire airplane with glass cleaner.

During this cleanup, inspect the covering for dings and dents. If the plane is covered with heat-shrink film, cure dents by applying heat to the affected areas. A small tear can be covered with a patch of the same material. But what about more serious dings?—the ones that cause minor structural damage.

The Leading Edge

Wing leading edges are probably subjected to the most damage. Posts, trees, stumps and

the covering is still well-bonded to the framework. Don't leave areas of unsupported covering, because they won't make good bonding points for the replacement covering when the repair is complete. When you've exposed the damaged areas, begin the repairs.

Whenever splices are made in wood, cut the two pieces to be joined so that there's as much gluing area as possible, i.e., cut both pieces at matching angles of 45 degrees or less. Cut away the damaged area of the leading edge at an angle slanting toward the damage on each side. If sheeting is involved, trim away the damaged sheet the same way—again, at an angle.

In some cases, you can use the material that's cut away as a template for shaping the replacement; this is especially true of sheeting. For the leading edge, however, its replacement is a cut-and-fit proposition. This isn't as difficult as it sounds. Cut the replacement slightly oversize, hold it just below the position it will occupy, and trim it a little at a time until you have a good fit. Use a gap-filling cement to take care of any spaces. When the new material has been cemented into place, sand it to match the old structure. (Use a sanding block and 150- to 320-grit sandpaper.)

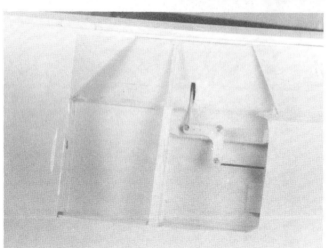

Above: A properly executed repair blends in with the rest of the wing—even when transparent covering is used!

Left: The same principle of angled cuts applies to the replacement of sheeted areas. This trailing-edge sheet was attacked by an unruly trunk lid!

Cut the replacement covering material so that it's at least 1/8 inch larger all around than the area to be covered. Position it, then iron it onto the spars, ribs and leading edge. Shrink it from the center outward, and try to avoid putting heat on the overlapping material. Cover the top and bottom with separate pieces of film. Check the seams; if any have risen, iron them back into place.

● **Fins and stabilizers** can be repaired the same way; just remember to angle all splices so that there's plenty of gluing area, and the joints will be good ones.

● **Ribs**. Although most damage occurs between ribs, a rib is occasionally involved. When this happens, it's very handy to have a template of the rib so you can make a duplicate, so whenever you build a new airplane, make an extra rib and put it aside for just such an emergency!

● **Foam wings.** The methods described for built-up wings also apply to foam wings; the only difference is that you trim a solid-foam wedge to fit the damaged section that's cut from the leading edge. If the wing is sheeted with balsa, the replaced foam is sanded to shape and covered with balsa sheet. On foam, always use white glue or aliphatic resin glue. Epoxy will work, but it's quite heavy.

Of course there's always a chance that having read the rest of this book, you'll never crash, but you need to know all this, just in case…! ■

Above: The parallel edges of a ruler make a good cutting template for replacement sheet. One side of the ruler is laid against the cut that's to be matched, and the sheet is trimmed along the other side.

Below: The new sheet is in place and ready to be glued. Use gap-filling glue and sandpaper to blend the repaired section into the rest of the wing.

Remember these tips

I admit that the title of this chapter is a little strange. It in no way implies that you don't need to know the information given in the other chapters, but it reflects my inability to come up with a better description of what you're about to read. Here are some tips that I just couldn't leave out of a book meant for beginners.

Sandpaper

Even if two pieces of sandpaper have the same grit size, it doesn't mean that they'll do the same job. To sand wood, use only garnet or aluminum-oxide paper, and make sure it says "open coat" on its reverse side. Open-coat paper is designed to release dust; it doesn't clog, but continues to cut, and good sandpaper does cut! Even the 400- and 600-grit papers will remove material efficiently.

Waterproof Glue

Unlike glue that's merely water-resistant, waterproof glue is supposed to withstand boiling water for a given time; whereas water-resistant glue withstands soaking for the same time period. Aliphatic-resin glue is easier to sand than CA (cyanoacrylate), and both are water-resistant. Model-airplane cement (Ambroid or Testors) is the easiest to sand!

Drilling Balsa

When you drill through balsa sheet, always put another piece of wood behind the area to be drilled so that the back of the wood you're drilling won't splinter. The sharper the drill, the cleaner the hole and the less splintering. Balsa tends to stick to dull drills, and this can result in a fuzzy hole with the wrong diameter. Large drills tend to "hog-out" the soft wood. Rather than drill a smooth, smaller hole, drill a smaller hole, and finish it by sanding with a dowel wrapped in sandpaper.

Fuel Tanks

Fuel tanks that have been wedged into place with foam have fewer fuel-foaming problems, and they're much easier to remove and re-

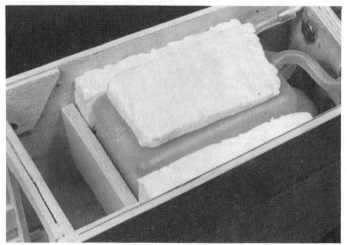

Foam pads around the fuel tank help to keep it in place and reduce fuel foaming.

Servo grommets should be checked often and replaced before they become too firm.

place. Fuel lines must be free of kinks. Use some sort of "strain relief" between the throttle arm and the servo. Epoxy glue should be used in any area that might be exposed to raw fuel and also to seal the seams of iron-on coverings near the engine and firewall.

Trailing-Edge Protection

Music wire epoxied to the wing's trailing edge at the center section prevents rubber bands from cutting into the wood. To eliminate a shear line, cross the wing rubber bands diagonally from side-to-side. After a flying session, put oiled rubber bands into a can of cat litter, and shake them to restore their elasticity. To eliminate exhaust saturation, paint the wing-holding dowels with epoxy paint.

Grommets & Batteries

Under compression, servo grommets eventually become hard and useless, so they must be replaced regularly. Mount servos with broad-head screws or with washers against the grommets, and recharge all your batteries after every flying session. Check receiving antennas for abrasions where they exit the fuselage, and repair them with heat-shrink tubing, if necessary.

Control Linkages

When you set up control linkages, remember that more force is applied to the surface when the servo pulls it than when it pushes it. The Nyrods should be anchored every 6 or 7 inches along their length and, to eliminate as much flexing as possible, the exit should be as close to the control horn as is practical. Use the rubber sleeve that comes with the clevises to secure them in the control horns. Manually wiggle all the control surfaces to check for any slop that might

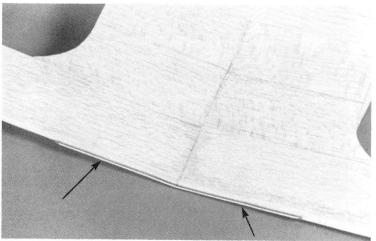

Music-wire implants at the wing center-section trailing edges prevent the rubber bands from damaging the wood.

cause flutter, and correct it if necessary.

Preflight & Post-Flight

A prop in which there are hairline cracks or chips will have to be replaced.

Before starting your engine, look behind the airplane to see whether the slipstream or exhaust will harm other fliers or their equipment.

Check control response before every flight, and after each flight, wipe the exhaust residue from the airplane and cover the engine. At the end of each session, remove exhaust residue with window cleaner and a paper towel.

To clean the engine, apply Marvel Mystery oil or automatic transmission fluid to the intake and exhaust ports. Turn the prop to work the oil into the engine, and cover it before storage.

Don't be afraid to ask for help! The only stupid questions are those that are never asked. ∎

Some sort of "strain relief" should be used in throttle lines. A hairpin bend in this wire pushrod does the job.

Oldies but goodies

When an AMA district vice president conducted an exhaustive study of airplane transmitters, he discovered something very interesting: transmitters sold 10, 15 and even 20 years ago (mostly AM and American-made) were well within the so-called "narrow-band" guidelines established by the AMA. Most transmitters (imported) sold since the late '70s were not! It's time for more American manufacturers to get back into the R/C business with their "old" designs.

Engine Protection

Much of the wear our poor engines suffer from occurs when they're started over dusty ground. To protect them, just put a piece of carpet under an airplane when it's being fueled.

While the engine is running and the plane is on the ground, the propeller creates a whirlwind right under the engine, and it can suck dirt into the air intake. Air cleaners that cover the air intake work well, but few use them because they make it difficult to choke or prime the engine. The next best thing is a piece of carpet laid fuzzy side down between the engine and the dirt.

Filter Systems

Sanding creates a lot of dust, which isn't good to breathe! A sanding booth with an exhaust fan and a dust collector would be great, but it's expensive. As an alternative, tape an air-conditioner filter to the back of a box fan. Set the fan on the bench with the filter toward the sanding job, and let it run while you're sanding. The filter will collect most of the sanding dust before it reaches the fan blades and your lungs. This fan-filter system also works fairly well for those who are allergic to the superglues. There's only one drawback: it's a little cold in an unheated shop in the winter.

Balsa Strippers

Balsa strippers have been around as long as there has been wood to strip. Although a large assortment of strips is available in most hobby shops, it's difficult to pick two identical pieces from a big bundle. Enter the stripper. If wing

Above: Flying fields aren't carpeted, so bring your own!

Below: An adjustable balsa stripper will soon pay for itself.

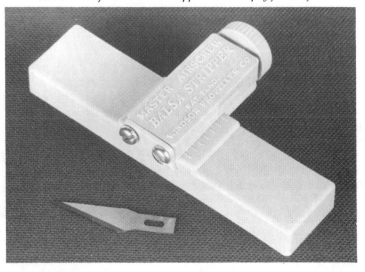

spars or fuselage longerons are stripped side-by-side from the same sheet of wood, they're as close to being matched as is practical.

Adjustable strippers can be used to make strips as small as $1/32$ inch square and as large as $1/4$ x $1/2$ inch. Remember to keep the sole of the stripper tight against the edge of the sheet being stripped, and strip over a smooth, hard surface. Every builder should have a balsa stripper and should know how to use one. Like the razor knife and the straightedge, it's an important tool. A small plan can be enlarged four times by cross-hatching it with $1/8$-inch squares and then drawing another grid with $1/2$-inch squares. When a number of points have been located on the larger grid, it's easy to draw the new, larger plan. This system works for wing ribs, bulkheads, formers and whole plans.

It's a lot easier to order full-size plans, but it isn't necessary if you have the time to enlarge the reduced-scale plans that are included with construction articles. Usually, a scale of inches is included with the plans, so you can figure out the size of the grid squares needed to draw full-size plans. A drawing board, a T-square and a triangle are essential tools for this part of the hobby.

Grids

Using a grid is probably the oldest way to enlarge plans or parts. You can cross-hatch a small plan with a series of accurately drawn squares and then, on another sheet, draw a grid with squares that are three or four times larger. Locate points on the small plan by counting squares, and mark them on the larger grid by counting in the same way. To complete the enlargement, connect the points on the large-scale grid with lines or curves.

A small plan can be enlarged four times by cross-hatching it with $1/8$-inch squares and then drawing another grid with $1/2$-inch squares. When a number of points have been located on the larger grid, it's easy to draw the new, larger plan. This system works for wing ribs, bulkheads, formers and whole plans.

It's a lot easier to order full-size plans, but it isn't necessary if you have the time to enlarge the reduced-scale plans that are included with construction articles. Usually, a scale of inches is included with the plans, so you can figure out the size of the grid squares needed to draw full-size plans. A drawing board, a T-square and a triangle are essential tools for this part of the hobby.

Someone once said, "There's nothing new under the sun," and they were almost right! ■

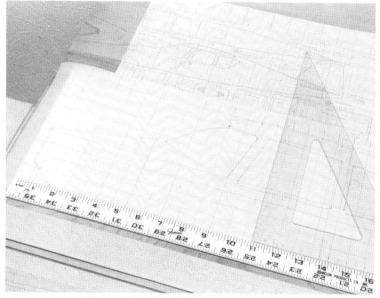

Plans can be enlarged. This is one way to do it.

Using new technology

In the chapter called "Comparing Airplanes," I described a computer program I use to compare the performances of airplanes. I wrote about the program in *Model Airplane News*, but since it's written in Atari 8-bit Basic, I didn't expect much response. Boy, was I mistaken!

Since most Basic languages are similar, it wasn't difficult for owners of other computers to rewrite it to suit their machines. People with all kinds of hardware sent for a copy of the printout.

The program gives numbers for a simple formula that gives some indication of flying speed, along with the other parameters. These lines were added to the original program and add one more aspect to be considered.

There are a number of factors that enter into calculations of the speed of an airplane. In tests run on five airplanes, the numbers the program returned were surprisingly close to the actual cruising speeds of the airplanes tested.

Aceing It!

I've mentioned Ace Radio so often that I've been accused of bias, but that isn't exactly the case! The Heathkit people have dominated the radio, television, audio and computer kit business for many years, and the same is true of Ace in its specialty—model hobby electronics. Ace produces quality products at reasonable prices.

One of the best ways to understand how a radio system works is by building one! That is a rather tall order, and it would be difficult for many to accomplish. Building a small part of a system is much less difficult and the chances of success are better. The picture shows one of Ace Radio's inexpensive servo kits, which is an excellent way to get acquainted with the system.

The servo is the "muscle" of the control system, and it's the device that changes the transmitted pulse into the movement that causes control surfaces to react to our commands. Inside that small box is an amplifier that builds the signal it receives to the strength necessary to drive an electric motor, which pro-

This is how an Ace servo kit looks when it comes out of the package. The instruction sheet tells you how to get it all into the case!

vides the actual movement.

The motor is connected through a series of gears to the output arm as well as to a circuit that tells the motor when it has moved in the right direction and when it has moved as far as it was told by the transmitter. There are many good things in that small package.

The other picture shows an example of what the servos move! The connection of flight surfaces to the servos is usually by way of pushrods—in this case, a flexible rod inside a sheath called a "Nyrod." The pushrod exit is above the elevator to ensure full servo strength (pull) for nose-up trim. When it encounters too much resistance to the "push" part of its function, this type of pushrod can flex if the sheath isn't anchored at several points inside the fuselage. Use this type of linkage so that it pulls the critical control in the critical direction.

These are just a few of the new goodies available to us; sure beats the days of rubber-band free-flight! ∎

Nyrods give us an easy way to transfer servo movement to control surfaces, but there are a few things to remember.

INDEX OF MANUFACTURERS

Ace RC
distributed by Ace Hobby
Distributors
2055 Main St.
Irvine, CA 92614
acehobby.com

Carl Goldberg Models
4734 West Chicago Ave.
Chicago, IL 60651
goldbergmodels.com

Cox Hobbies
P.O. Box 270
Penrose, CO 81240
estesrockets.com

Dynaflite
1578 Osage
San Marcos, CA 92069
dynaflite.com

Experimental Aircraft Association
P.O. Box 3086
Oshkosh, WI 54903
eea.org

Futaba
distributed by Great Planes
futaba-rc.com

Great Planes Model Distributors
2904 Research Rd.
P.O. Box 9021
Champaign, IL 61826-9021
greatplanes.com

Hot Stuff/Satellite City
P.O. Box 836
Simi, CA 93062

J'Tec
660 Pacific Ave.
Oxnard, CA 93030
jtecrc.com

Lanier RC
P.O. Box 458, Oakwood Rd.
Oakwood, GA 30566
lanierrc.com

Marvel Mystery Oil
Available at your automotive
supply store.

MRC (Model Rectifier Corp.)
P.O. Box 6312
Edison, NJ 08837
modelrectifier.com

Pacer Technology
9420 Santa Anita Ave.
Rancho Cucamonga, CA 91730
pacertechnology.com

RPM R/C Products
14978 Sierra Bonita Ln.
P.O. Box 836
Chino, CA 91710
rpmrcproducts.com

Sig Mfg. Co.
401 S. Front St.
Montezuma, IA 50171
sigmfg.com

Super Jet, Super T/ Carl Goldberg Models
goldbergmodels.com

Tamiya America Inc.
2 Orion
Aliso Viejo, CA 92656-4200
tamiya.com

Testors Corp.
620 Buckbee St.
Rockford, IL 61104
testors.com